AUTOBIOGRAPHY

OF RED

AUTOBIOGRAPHY

OF RED

A Novel in Verse

A N N E C A R S O N

Alfred A. Knopf   New York   1998

Carson, Anne.
Autobiography of Red / by Anne Carson. — 1st ed.
p.   cm.
ISBN 0-375-40133-4
1. Herakles (Greek mythology)—Poetry.   2. Stesichoros.
Geryoneis—Adaptations.   3. Epic poetry, Greek—Adaptations.
4. Monsters—Mythology—Poetry.   I. Title.
PS3553.A7667A94   1998
811'.54—dc21   97-49472   CIP

FOR WILL

CONTENTS

AUTOBIOGRAPHY

OF RED

RED MEAT:

WHAT DIFFERENCE

DID

STESICHOROS MAKE?

I like the feeling of words doing
as they want to do and as they have to do.

H E CAME after Homer and before Gertrude Stein, a diffi-
cult interval for a poet. Born about 650 B.C. on the north
coast of Sicily in a city called Himera, he lived among refugees who
spoke a mixed dialect of Chalcidian and Doric. A refugee population
is hungry for language and aware that anything can happen. Words
bounce. Words, if you let them, will do what they want to do and
what they have to do. Stesichoros' words were collected in twenty-
six books of which there remain to us a dozen or so titles and sev-
eral collections of fragments. Not much is known about his working
life (except the famous story that he was struck blind by Helen; see
Appendixes A, B, C). He seems to have had a great popular success.

How did the critics regard him? Many ancient praises adhere to his name. "Most Homeric of the lyric poets," says Longinus. "Makes those old stories new," says Suidas. "Driven by a craving for change," says Dionysios of Halikarnassos. "What a sweet genius in the use of adjectives!" adds Hermogenes. Here we touch the core of the question "What difference did Stesichoros make?" A comparison may be useful. When Gertrude Stein had to sum up Picasso she said, "This one was working." So say of Stesichoros, "This one was making adjectives."

What is an adjective? Nouns name the world. Verbs activate the names. Adjectives come from somewhere else. The word *adjective* (*epitheton* in Greek) is itself an adjective meaning "placed on top," "added," "appended," "imported," "foreign." Adjectives seem fairly innocent additions but look again. These small imported mechanisms are in charge of attaching everything in the world to its place in particularity. They are the latches of being.

Of course there are several different ways to be. In the world of the Homeric epic, for example, being is stable and particularity is set fast in tradition. When Homer mentions blood, blood is *black*. When women appear, women are *neat-ankled* or *glancing*. Poseidon always has *the blue eyebrows of Poseidon*. Gods' laughter is *unquenchable*. Human knees are *quick*. The sea is *unwearying*. Death is *bad*. Cowards' livers are *white*. Homer's epithets are a fixed diction with which Homer fastens every substance in the world to its aptest attribute and holds them in place for epic consumption. There is a passion in it but what kind of passion? "Consumption is not a passion for substances but a passion for the code," says Baudrillard.

So into the still surface of this code Stesichoros was born. And Stesichoros was studying the surface restlessly. It leaned away from him. He went closer. It stopped. "Passion for substances" seems a good description of that moment. For no reason that anyone can name, Stesichoros began to undo the latches.

Stesichoros released being. All the substances in the world went floating up. Suddenly there was nothing to interfere with horses being *hollow hooved*. Or a river being *root silver*. Or a child *bruiseless*. Or hell *as deep as the sun is high*. Or Herakles *ordeal strong*. Or a planet *middle night stuck*. Or an insomniac *outside the joy*. Or killings *cream black*. Some substances proved more complex. To Helen of Troy, for example, was attached an adjectival tradition of whoredom already old by the time Homer used it. When Stesichoros unlatched her epithet from Helen there flowed out such a light as may have blinded him for a moment. This is a big question, the question of the blinding of Stesichoros by Helen (see Appendixes A, B), although generally regarded as unanswerable (but see Appendix C).

A more tractable example is Geryon. Geryon is the name of a character in ancient Greek myth about whom Stesichoros wrote a very long lyric poem in dactylo-epitrite meter and triadic structure. Some eighty-four papyrus fragments and a half-dozen citations survive, which go by the name *Geryoneis* ("The Geryon Matter") in standard editions. They tell of a strange winged red monster who lived on an island called Erytheia (which is an adjective meaning simply "The Red Place") quietly tending a herd of magical red cattle, until one day the hero Herakles came across the sea and killed him to get the cattle. There were many different ways to tell a story like this.

Herakles was an important Greek hero and the elimination of Geryon constituted one of His celebrated Labors. If Stesichoros had been a more conventional poet he might have taken the point of view of Herakles and framed a thrilling account of the victory of culture over monstrosity. But instead the extant fragments of Stesichoros' poem offer a tantalizing cross section of scenes, both proud and pitiful, from Geryon's own experience. We see his red boy's life and his little dog. A scene of wild appeal from his mother, which breaks off. Interspersed shots of Herakles approaching over the sea. A flash of the gods in heaven pointing to Geryon's doom. The battle itself. The moment when everything goes suddenly slow and Herakles' arrow divides Geryon's skull. We see Herakles kill the little dog with His famous club.

But that is enough proemium. You can answer for yourself the question "What difference did Stesichoros make?" by considering his masterpiece. Some of its principal fragments are below. If you find the text difficult, you are not alone. Time has dealt harshly with Stesichoros. No passage longer than thirty lines is quoted from him and papyrus scraps (still being found: the most recent fragments were recovered from cartonnage in Egypt in 1977) withhold as much as they tell. The whole corpus of the fragments of Stesichoros in the original Greek has been published thirteen times so far by different editors, beginning with Bergk in 1882. No edition is exactly the same as any other in its contents or its ordering of the contents. Bergk says the history of a text is like a long caress. However that may be, the fragments of the *Geryoneis* itself read as if Stesichoros had composed a substantial narrative poem then ripped it to pieces and buried the pieces in a box with some song lyrics and lecture notes and scraps of meat. The fragment numbers tell you roughly how the pieces fell out of the box. You can of course keep shaking the box. "Believe me for meat and for myself," as Gertrude Stein says. Here. Shake.

RED MEAT:

FRAGMENTS OF STESICHOROS

I. GERYON

Geryon was a monster everything about him was red

Put his snout out of the covers in the morning it was red

How stiff the red landscape where his cattle scraped against

Their hobbles in the red wind

Burrowed himself down in the red dawn jelly of Geryon's

Dream

Geryon's dream began red then slipped out of the vat and ran

Upsail broke silver shot up through his roots like a pup

Secret pup At the front end of another red day

II. MEANWHILE HE CAME

Across the salt knobs it was Him

Knew about the homegold

Had sighted red smoke above the red spires

III. GERYON'S PARENTS

If you persist in wearing your mask at the supper table

Well Goodnight Then they said and drove him up

Those hemorrhaging stairs to the hot dry Arms

To the ticking red taxi of the incubus

Don't want to go want to stay Downstairs and read

IV. GERYON'S DEATH BEGINS

Geryon walked the red length of his mind and answered No

It was murder And torn to see the cattle lay

All these darlings said Geryon And now me

V. GERYON'S REVERSIBLE DESTINY

His mother saw it mothers are like that

Trust me she said Engineer of his softness

You don't have to make up your mind right away

Behind her red right cheek Geryon could see

Coil of the hot plate starting to glow

VI. MEANWHILE IN HEAVEN

Athena was looking down through the floor

Of the glass-bottomed boat Athena pointed

Zeus looked *Him*

VII. GERYON'S WEEKEND

Later well later they left the bar went back to the centaur's

Place the centaur had a cup made out of a skull Holding three

Measures of wine Holding it he drank Come over here you can

Bring your drink if you're afraid to come alone The centaur

Patted the sofa beside him Reddish yellow small alive animal

Not a bee moved up Geryon's spine on the inside

VIII. GERYON'S FATHER

A quiet root may know how to holler He liked to

Suck words Here is an almighty one he would say

After days of standing in the doorway

NIGHTBOLLSNORTED

IX. GERYON'S WAR RECORD

Geryon lay on the ground covering his ears The sound
Of the horses like roses being burned alive

X. SCHOOLING

In those days the police were weak Family was strong
Hand in hand the first day Geryon's mother took him to
School She neatened his little red wings and pushed him
In through the door

XI. RIGHT

Are there many little boys who think they are a
Monster? But in my case I am right said Geryon to the
Dog they were sitting on the bluffs The dog regarded him
Joyfully

XII. WINGS

Steps off a scraped March sky and sinks

Up into the blind Atlantic morning One small

Red dog jumping across the beach miles below

Like a freed shadow

XIII. HERAKLES' KILLING CLUB

Little red dog did not see it he felt it All

Events carry but one

XIV. HERAKLES' ARROW

Arrow means kill It parted Geryon's skull like a comb Made

The boy neck lean At an odd slow angle sideways as when a

Poppy shames itself in a whip of Nude breeze

XV. TOTAL THINGS KNOWN
ABOUT GERYON

He loved lightning He lived on an island His mother was a
Nymph of a river that ran to the sea His father was a gold
Cutting tool Old scholia say that Stesichoros says that
Geryon had six hands and six feet and wings He was red and
His strange red cattle excited envy Herakles came and
Killed him for his cattle

The dog too

XVI. GERYON'S END

The red world And corresponding red breezes
Went on Geryon did not

APPENDIX A

———————

Suidas s.v. *palinodia:* "Counter song" or "saying the opposite of what you said before." E.g., for writing abuse of Helen Stesichoros was struck blind but then he wrote for her an encomium and got his sight back. The encomium came out of a dream and is called "The Palinode."

Isokrates *Helen* 64: Looking to demonstrate her own power Helen made an object lesson of the poet Stesichoros. For the fact is he began his poem "Helen" with a bit of blasphemy. Then when he stood up he found he'd been robbed of his eyes. Straightaway realizing why, he composed the so-called "Palinode" and Helen restored him to his own nature.

Plato *Phaedrus* 243a: There is in mythology an ancient tactic of purgation for criminals, which Homer did not understand but Stesichoros did. When Stesichoros found himself blinded for slandering Helen he did not (like Homer) just stand there bewildered—no! on the contrary. Stesichoros was an intellectual. He recognized the cause and at once sat down to compose [his "Palinode"]. . . .

APPENDIX B

=========

THE   PALINODE

OF

STESICHOROS

BY

STESICHOROS

(FRAGMENT

192   *POETAE MELICI*

GRAECI)

No it is not the true story.
No you never went on the benched ships.
No you never came to the towers of Troy.

/ / / / / / /

17

APPENDIX C

CLEARING UP

THE QUESTION OF

STESICHOROS' BLINDING

BY HELEN

1. Either Stesichoros was a blind man or he was not.

2. If Stesichoros was a blind man either his blindness was a temporary condition or it was permanent.

3. If Stesichoros' blindness was a temporary condition this condition either had a contingent cause or it had none.

4. If this condition had a contingent cause that cause was Helen or the cause was not Helen.

5. If the cause was Helen Helen had her reasons or she had none.

6. If Helen had her reasons the reasons arose out of some remark Stesichoros made or they did not.

7. If Helen's reasons arose out of some remark Stesichoros made either it was a strong remark about Helen's sexual misconduct (not to say its unsavory aftermath the Fall of Troy) or it was not.

8. If it was a strong remark about Helen's sexual misconduct (not to say its unsavory aftermath the Fall of Troy) either this remark was a lie or it was not.

9. If it was not a lie either we are now in reverse and by continuing to reason in this way are likely to arrive back at the beginning of the question of the blinding of Stesichoros or we are not.

10. If we are now in reverse and by continuing to reason in this way are likely to arrive back at the beginning of the question of the blinding of Stesichoros either we will go along without incident or we will meet Stesichoros on our way back.

11. If we meet Stesichoros on our way back either we will keep quiet or we will look him in the eye and ask him what he thinks of Helen.

12. If we look Stesichoros in the eye and ask him what he thinks of Helen either he will tell the truth or he will lie.

13. If Stesichoros lies either we will know at once that he is lying or we will be fooled because now that we are in reverse the whole landscape looks inside out.

14. If we are fooled because now that we are in reverse the whole land-
    scape looks inside out either we will find that we do not have a sin-
    gle penny on us or we will call Helen up and tell her the good news.

15. If we call Helen up either she will sit with her glass of vermouth and
    let it ring or she will answer.

16. If she answers either we will (as they say) leave well enough alone or
    we will put Stesichoros on.

17. If we put Stesichoros on either he will contend that he now sees
    more clearly than ever before the truth about her whoring or he will
    admit he is a liar.

18. If Stesichoros admits he is a liar either we will melt into the crowd or
    we will stay to see how Helen reacts.

19. If we stay to see how Helen reacts either we will find ourselves pleas-
    antly surprised by her dialectical abilities or we will be taken down-
    town by the police for questioning.

20. If we are taken downtown by the police for questioning either we
    will be expected (as eyewitnesses) to clear up once and for all the
    question whether Stesichoros was a blind man or not.

21. If Stesichoros was a blind man either we will lie or if not not.

AUTOBIOGRAPHY

OF RED

_____

A ROMANCE

The reticent volcano keeps

His never slumbering plan—

Confided are his projects pink

To no precarious man.

If nature will not tell the tale

Jehovah told to her

Can human nature not survive

Without a listener?

Admonished by her buckled lips

Let every babbler be

The only secret people keep

Is Immortality.

EMILY DICKINSON,

NO. 1748

I. JUSTICE

Geryon learned about justice from his brother quite early.

They used to go to school together. Geryon's brother was bigger and older,

he walked in front

sometimes broke into a run or dropped on one knee to pick up a stone.

Stones make my brother happy,

thought Geryon and he studied stones as he trotted along behind.

So many different kinds of stones,

the sober and the uncanny, lying side by side in the red dirt.

To stop and imagine the life of each one!

Now they were sailing through the air from a happy human arm,

what a fate. Geryon hurried on.

Arrived at the schoolyard. He was focusing hard on his feet and his steps.

Children poured around him

and the intolerable red assault of grass and the smell of grass everywhere

was pulling him towards it

like a strong sea. He could feel his eyes leaning out of his skull

on their little connectors.

He had to make it to the door. He had to not lose track of his brother.

These two things.

School was a long brick building on a north–south axis. South: Main Door

through which all boys and girls must enter.

North: Kindergarten, its large round windows gazing onto the backwoods

and surrounded by a hedge of highbush cranberry.

Between Main Door and Kindergarten ran a corridor. To Geryon it was a hundred thousand miles

of thunder tunnels and indoor neon sky slammed open by giants.

Hand in hand on the first day of school

Geryon crossed this alien terrain with his mother. Then his brother

performed the task day after day.

But as September moved into October an unrest was growing in Geryon's brother.

Geryon had always been stupid

but nowadays the look in his eyes made a person feel strange.

Just take me once more I'll get it this time,

Geryon would say. The eyes terrible holes. *Stupid,* said Geryon's brother

and left him.

Geryon had no doubt *stupid* was correct. But when justice is done

the world drops away.

He stood on his small red shadow and thought what to do next.

Main Door rose before him. Perhaps—

peering hard Geryon made his way through the fires in his mind to where

the map should be.

In place of a map of the school corridor lay a deep glowing blank.

Geryon's anger was total.

The blank caught fire and burned to baseline. Geryon ran.

After that Geryon went to school alone.

He did not approach Main Door at all. Justice is pure. He would make his way

around the long brick sidewall,

past the windows of Seventh Grade, Fourth Grade, Second Grade and Boys'

to the north end of the school

and position himself in the bushes outside Kindergarten. There he would stand

motionless

until someone inside noticed and came out to show him the way.

He did not gesticulate.

He did not knock on the glass. He waited. Small, red, and upright he waited,

gripping his new bookbag tight

in one hand and touching a lucky penny inside his coat pocket with the other,

while the first snows of winter

floated down on his eyelashes and covered the branches around him and silenced

all trace of the world.

II. EACH

Like honey is the sleep of the just.

———

When Geryon was little he loved to sleep but even more he loved to wake up.
He would run outside in his pajamas.
Hard morning winds were blowing life bolts against the sky each one blue enough
to begin a world of its own.
The word *each* blew towards him and came apart on the wind. Geryon had always
had this trouble: a word like *each,*
when he stared at it, would disassemble itself into separate letters and go.
A space for its meaning remained there but blank.
The letters themselves could be found hung on branches or furniture in the area.
What does each *mean?*
Geryon had asked his mother. She never lied to him. Once she said the meaning
it would stay.
She answered, Each *means like you and your brother each have your own room.*
He clothed himself in this strong word *each.*
He spelled it at school on the blackboard (perfectly) with a piece of red silk chalk.
He thought softly
of other words he could keep with him like *beach* and *screach.* Then they moved
Geryon into his brother's room.
It happened by accident. Geryon's grandmother came to visit and fell off the bus.
The doctors put her together again
with a big silver pin. Then she and her pin had to lie still in Geryon's room
for many months. So began Geryon's nightlife.
Before this time Geryon had not lived nights just days and their red intervals.

What's that smell in your room? asked Geryon.

Geryon and his brother were lying in the dark in their bunk beds Geryon on top.

When Geryon moved his arms or legs

the bedsprings made an enjoyable PING SHUNK SHUNK PING enclosing him from below

like a thick clean bandage.

There's no smell in my room, said Geryon's brother. *Maybe it's your socks,*

or the frog did you

bring the frog in? said Geryon. *What smells in here is you Geryon.*

Geryon paused.

He had a respect for facts maybe this was one. Then he heard

a different sound from below.

SHUNK SHUNK PING PING PING PING PING PING PING PING PING PING PING PING

PING PING PING PING PING PING PING PING PING.

His brother was pulling on his stick as he did most nights before sleep.

Why do you pull on your stick?

Geryon asked. *None of your business let's see yours,* said his brother.

No.

Bet you don't have one. Geryon checked. *Yes I do.*

You're so ugly I bet it fell off.

Geryon remained silent. He knew the difference between facts and brother hatred.

Show me yours

and I'll give you something good, said Geryon's brother.

No.

Give you one of my cat's-eyes.

No you won't.

I will.

Don't believe you.

Promise.

Now Geryon very much wanted a cat's-eye. He never could win a cat's-eye when he

knelt on cold knees

on the basement floor to shoot marbles with his brother and his brother's friends.
A cat's-eye

is outranked only by a steelie. And so they developed an economy of sex

for cat's-eyes.

Pulling the stick makes my brother happy, thought Geryon. *Don't tell Mom,*

said his brother.

Voyaging into the rotten ruby of the night became a contest of freedom

and bad logic.

Come on Geryon.

No.

You owe me.

No.

I hate you. I don't care. I'll tell Mom. Tell Mom what?

How nobody likes you at school.

Geryon paused. Facts are bigger in the dark. Sometimes then he would descend

to the other bunk

and let his brother do what he liked or else hang in between with his face pressed

into the edge of his own mattress,

cold toes balancing on the bed below. After it was over his brother's voice

got very kind.

You're nice Geryon I'll take you swimming tomorrow okay?

Geryon would climb back up to his bunk,

recover his pajama bottoms and lie on his back. He lay very straight

in the fantastic temperatures

of the red pulse as it sank away and he thought about the difference

between outside and inside.

Inside is mine, he thought. The next day Geryon and his brother

went to the beach.

They swam and practiced belching and ate jam-and-sand sandwiches on a blanket.

Geryon's brother found an American dollar bill

and gave it to Geryon. Geryon found a piece of an old war helmet and hid it.

That was also the day

he began his autobiography. In this work Geryon set down all inside things

particularly his own heroism

and early death much to the despair of the community. He coolly omitted

all outside things.

III. RHINESTONES

Geryon straightened and put his hands quick under the table, not quick enough.

———

Don't pick at that Geryon you'll get it infected. Just leave it alone and let it heal,
said his mother

rhinestoning past on her way to the door. She had all her breasts on this evening.
Geryon stared in amazement.

She looked so brave. He could look at her forever. But now she was at the door
and then she was gone.

Geryon felt the walls of the kitchen contract as most of the air in the room
swirled after her.

He could not breathe. He knew he must not cry. And he knew the sound
of the door closing

had to be kept out of him. Geryon turned all attention to his inside world.
Just then his brother came into the kitchen.

Want to wrestle? said Geryon's brother.

No, said Geryon.

Why? Just don't. Oh come on. Geryon's brother picked up
the empty tin fruit bowl

from the kitchen table and placed it upside down over Geryon's head.

What time is it?

Geryon's voice came muffled from inside the fruit bowl. *Can't tell you,* said his brother.

Please.

Look for yourself. I don't want to. You mean you can't.

The fruit bowl was very still.

You're so stupid you can't tell time can you? How old are you anyway? What a jerk.

Can you tie your shoes yet?

The fruit bowl paused. Geryon could in fact tie knots but not bows.

He chose to pass over this distinction.

Yes.

Suddenly Geryon's brother stepped behind Geryon and seized him by the neck.

This is the silent death hold,

Geryon, in war they use this for knocking out all sentries. With one surprise twist

I can break your neck.

They heard the baby-sitter approaching and Geryon's brother stepped quickly away.

Is Geryon sulking again?

said the baby-sitter entering the kitchen. *No,* said the fruit bowl.

Geryon very much wanted

to keep the baby-sitter's voice out of him. In fact he would have preferred

not to know her at all

but there was one piece of information he needed to get.

What time is it?

he heard himself ask. *Quarter to eight,* she answered. *What time will Mom be home?*

Oh not for hours yet,

eleven maybe. At this news Geryon felt everything in the room hurl itself

away from him

towards the rims of the world. Meanwhile the baby-sitter continued,

You better start getting ready for bed, Geryon.

She was taking the fruit bowl off Geryon's head and moving towards the sink.

Do you want me to read to you?

Your mom says you have trouble going to sleep. What do you like to read?

Bits of words drifted past Geryon's brain like ash.

He knew he would have to let the baby-sitter go through with this in her wrong voice.

She was standing before him now

smiling hard and rummaging in his face with her eyes. *Read the loon book,* he said.

This was cagey.

The loon book was an instruction manual for calling loons. At least

it would keep her wrong voice away

from words that belonged to his mother. The baby-sitter went off happily

to find the loon book.

A while later the baby-sitter and Geryon were sitting on the top bunk calling loons

when Geryon's brother surged in

and landed on the lower bunk, bouncing everyone up to the ceiling.

Geryon drew back

against the wall with his knees up as his brother's head appeared,

then the rest of him.

He clambered into place beside Geryon. He had a thick rubber band

stretched between his thumb

and index finger which he snapped on Geryon's leg. *What's your favorite weapon?*

Mine's the catapult BLAM—

he snapped Geryon's leg again—*you can wipe out the whole downtown*

with a catapult surprise attack BLAM—

everyone dead or else fill it with incendiaries like Alexander the Great he

invented the catapult

Alexander the Great personally BLAM— *Stop that,*

said the baby-sitter

grabbing for the rubber band. She missed. Pushing her glasses back up

onto her nose she said, *Garotte.*

I like the garotte best. It is clean and neat. An Italian invention I believe

although the word is French.

What's a garotte? asked Geryon's brother. Taking the rubber band from his thumb
she shoved it in her shirt pocket and said,

A short piece of cord usually silk with a slipknot in one end. You put it
around someone's neck

from behind and pull tight. Cuts off the windpipe. Quick but painful death.

No noise no blood

no bulge in your pocket. Murderers on trains use them.

Geryon's brother was regarding her with one eye closed his mode of total attention.

What about you Geryon

what's your favorite weapon? Cage, said Geryon from behind his knees.

Cage? said his brother.

You idiot a cage isn't a weapon. It has to do something to be a weapon.

Has to destroy the enemy.

Just then there was a loud noise downstairs. Inside Geryon something burst into flame.

He hit the floor running. *Mom!*

IV. TUESDAY

Tuesdays were best.

———

Every second Tuesday in winter Geryon's father and brother went to hockey practice.
Geryon and his mother had supper alone.
They grinned at each other as night climbed ashore. Turned on all the lights
even in rooms they weren't using.
Geryon's mother made their favorite meal, cling peaches from the can and toast
cut into fingers for dipping.
Lots of butter on the toast so a little oil slick floats out on top of the peach juice.
They took supper trays into the living room.
Geryon's mother sat on the rug with magazines, cigarettes, and telephone.
Geryon worked beside her under the lamp.
He was gluing a cigarette to a tomato. *Don't pick your lip Geryon let it heal.*
She blew smoke out her nose
as she dialed. *Maria? It's me can you talk? What did he say?*

. . . .

Just like that?

. . . .

Bastard

. . . .

That's not freedom it's indifference

. . . .

Some kind of addict

. . . .

I'd throw the bum out

. . . .

/ / / / / / / /

*That's melodrama—*she stubbed her cigarette hard—*why not have a nice bath*

. . . .

Yes dear I know it doesn't matter now

. . . .

Geryon? fine he's right here working on his autobiography

. . . .

No it's a sculpture he doesn't know how to write yet

. . . .

Oh this and that stuff he finds outside Geryon's always finding things
aren't you Geryon?

She winked at him over the telephone. He winked back using both eyes
and returned to work.

He had ripped up some pieces of crispy paper he found in her purse to use for hair
and was gluing these to the top of the tomato.

Outside the house a black January wind came flattening down from the top of the sky
and hit the windows hard.

The lamp flared. *It's beautiful Geryon,* she said hanging up the telephone.

It's a beautiful sculpture.

She put her hand on top of his small luminous skull as she studied the tomato.

And bending she kissed him once on each eye

then picked up her bowl of peaches from the tray and handed Geryon his.

Maybe next time you could

use a one-dollar bill instead of a ten for the hair, she said as they began to eat.

V. SCREENDOOR

His mother stood at the ironing board lighting a cigarette and regarding Geryon.

———————

Outside the dark pink air

was already hot and alive with cries. *Time to go to school,* she said for the third time.

Her cool voice floated

over a pile of fresh tea towels and across the shadowy kitchen to where Geryon stood

at the screen door.

He would remember when he was past forty the dusty almost medieval smell

of the screen itself as it

pressed its grid onto his face. She was behind him now. *This would be hard*

for you if you were weak

but you're not weak, she said and neatened his little red wings and pushed him

out the door.

VI. IDEAS

Eventually Geryon learned to write.

———

His mother's friend Maria gave him a beautiful notebook from Japan
with a fluorescent cover.
On the cover Geryon wrote *Autobiography*. Inside he set down the facts.

> *Total Facts Known About Geryon.*
> *Geryon was a monster everything about him was red. Geryon lived*
> *on an island in the Atlantic called the Red Place. Geryon's mother*
> *was a river that runs to the sea the Red Joy River Geryon's father*
> *was gold. Some say Geryon had six hands six feet some say wings.*
> *Geryon was red so were his strange red cattle. Herakles came one*
> *day killed Geryon got the cattle.*

He followed Facts with Questions and Answers.

> QUESTIONS *Why did Herakles kill Geryon?*
> 1. *Just violent.*
> 2. *Had to it was one of His Labors (10th).*
> 3. *Got the idea that Geryon was Death otherwise he could live forever.*

> FINALLY
> *Geryon had a little red dog Herakles killed that too.*

Where does he get his ideas, said the teacher. It was Parent-Teacher Day at school.

They were sitting side by side in tiny desks.

Geryon watched his mother pick a fragment of tobacco off her tongue before she said,

Does he ever write anything with a happy ending?

Geryon paused.

Then he reached up and carefully disengaged the composition paper

from the teacher's hand.

Proceeding to the back of the classroom he sat at his usual desk and took out a pencil.

    New Ending.

    All over the world the beautiful red breezes went on blowing hand

    in hand.

VII. CHANGE

Somehow Geryon made it to adolescence.

———

Then he met Herakles and the kingdoms of his life all shifted down a few notches.

They were two superior eels

at the bottom of the tank and they recognized each other like italics.

Geryon was going into the Bus Depot

one Friday night about three a.m. to get change to call home. Herakles stepped off

the bus from New Mexico and Geryon

came fast around the corner of the platform and there it was one of those moments

that is the opposite of blindness.

The world poured back and forth between their eyes once or twice. Other people

wishing to disembark the bus from New Mexico

were jamming up behind Herakles who had stopped on the bottom step

with his suitcase in one hand

trying to tuck in his shirt with the other. *Do you have change for a dollar?*

Geryon heard Geryon say.

No. Herakles stared straight at Geryon. *But I'll give you a quarter for free.*

Why would you do that?

I believe in being gracious. Some hours later they were down

at the railroad tracks

standing close together by the switch lights. The huge night moved overhead

scattering drops of itself.

You're cold, said Herakles suddenly, *your hands are cold. Here.*

He put Geryon's hands inside his shirt.

VIII. CLICK

So who is this new kid you spend all your time with now?

———————

Geryon's mother turned to knock her cigarette ash on the sink then faced Geryon again.

He was seated at the kitchen table

with his camera in front of his face adjusting the focus. He did not answer.

He had recently relinquished speech.

His mother continued. *I hear he doesn't go to school, is he older?*

Geryon was focusing the camera on her throat.

Nobody sees him around, is it true he lives in the trailer park—that where you

go at night?

Geryon moved the focal ring from 3 to 3.5 meters.

Maybe I'll just keep talking

and if I say anything intelligent you can take a picture of it. She inhaled.

I don't trust people who

move around only at night. Exhaled. *Yet I trust you. I lie in bed at night thinking,*

Why didn't I

teach the kid something useful. Well—she took a last pull on the cigarette—

you probably know

more about sex than I do—and turned to stub it in the sink as he clicked the shutter.

A half laugh escaped her.

Geryon began to focus again, on her mouth. She leaned against the sink in silence

for some moments

gazing down the sight line into his lens. *Funny when you were a baby*

you were an insomniac

do you remember that? I'd go into your room at night and there you were

- - - - - - - -
40

in your crib lying on your back

with your eyes wide open. Staring into the dark. You never cried just stared.

You'd lie that way for hours

but if I took you in the TV room you were asleep in five minutes—Geryon's

camera swiveled left

as his brother came into the kitchen. *Going downtown want to come? Bring*

some money—

The words dropped behind him as he went banging out the screen door.

Geryon rose slowly,

closing the shutter release and pushing the camera into the pocket of his jacket.

Got your lens cap? she said as he moved past her.

IX. SPACE AND TIME

Up against another human being one's own procedures take on definition.

————

Geryon was amazed at himself. He saw Herakles just about every day now.
The instant of nature
forming between them drained every drop from the walls of his life
leaving behind just ghosts
rustling like an old map. He had nothing to say to anyone. He felt loose and shiny.
He burned in the presence of his mother.
I hardly know you anymore, she said leaning against the doorway of his room.
It had rained suddenly at suppertime,
now sunset was startling drops at the window. Stale peace of old bedtimes
filled the room. Love does not
make me gentle or kind, thought Geryon as he and his mother eyed each other
from opposite shores of the light.
He was filling his pockets with money, keys, film. She tapped a cigarette
on the back of her hand.
I put some clean T-shirts in your top drawer this afternoon, she said.
Her voice drew a circle
around all the years he had spent in this room. Geryon glanced down.
This one is clean, he said,
it's supposed to look this way. The T-shirt was ripped here and there.
GOD LOVES LOLA in red letters.
Glad she can't see the back, he thought as he shrugged on his jacket and stuck
the camera in the pocket.
What time will you be home? she said. *Not too late,* he answered.

/ / / / / / /

A pure bold longing to be gone filled him.

So Geryon what do you like about this guy this Herakles can you tell me?

Can I tell you, thought Geryon.

Thousand things he could not tell flowed over his mind. *Herakles knows a lot*

about art. We have good discussions.

She was looking not at him but past him as she stored the unlit cigarette

in her front shirt pocket.

"How does distance look?" is a simple direct question. It extends from a spaceless

within to the edge

of what can be loved. It depends on light. *Light that for you?* he said pulling

a book of matches

out of his jeans as he came towards her. *No thanks dear.* She was turning away.

I really should quit.

X. SEX QUESTION

Is it a question?

———

I better be getting home.

Okay.

They continued to sit. They were parked way out on the highway.

Cold night smell

coming in the windows. New moon floating white as a rib at the edge of the sky.

I guess I'm someone who will never be satisfied,

said Herakles. Geryon felt all nerves in him move to the surface of his body.

What do you mean satisfied?

Just—satisfied. I don't know. From far down the freeway came a sound

of fishhooks scraping the bottom of the world.

You know. Satisfied. Geryon was thinking hard. Fires twisted through him.

He picked his way carefully

toward the sex question. Why is it a question? He understood

that people need

acts of attention from one another, does it really matter which acts?

He was fourteen.

Sex is a way of getting to know someone,

Herakles had said. He was sixteen. Hot unsorted parts of the question

were licking up from every crack in Geryon,

he beat at them as a nervous laugh escaped him. Herakles looked.

Suddenly quiet.

It's okay, said Herakles. His voice washed

Geryon open.

Tell me, said Geryon and he intended to ask him, Do people who like sex

have a question about it too?

but the words came out wrong—*Is it true you think about sex every day?*

Herakles' body stiffened.

That isn't a question it's an accusation. Something black and heavy dropped

between them like a smell of velvet.

Herakles switched on the ignition and they jumped forward onto the back of the night.

Not touching

but joined in astonishment as two cuts lie parallel in the same flesh.

XI. HADES

Sometimes a journey makes itself necessary.

————

SPIRIT RULES SECRETLY ALONE THE BODY ACHIEVES NOTHING
is something you know
instinctively at fourteen and can still remember even with hell in your head
at sixteen. They painted this truth
on the long wall of the high school the night before departing for Hades.
Herakles' hometown of Hades
lay at the other end of the island about four hours by car, a town
of moderate size and little importance
except for one thing. *Have you ever seen a volcano?* said Herakles.
Staring at him Geryon felt his soul
move in his side. Then Geryon wrote a note full of lies for his mother
and stuck it on the fridge.
They climbed into Herakles' car and set off westward. Cold green summer night.
Active?
The volcano? Yes the last time she blew was 1923. Threw 180 cubic kilometers
of rock into the air
covered the countryside with fire overturned sixteen ships in the bay.
My grandmother says
the temperature of the air rose to seven hundred degrees centigrade downtown.
Caskets
of whiskey and rum burst into flame on the main street.
She saw it erupt?
Watched from the roof. Took a photograph of it, three p.m. looks like midnight.

/ / / / / / / /

What happened to the town?

Cooked. There was a survivor—prisoner in the local jail.

Wonder what happened to him.

You'll have to ask my grandmother about that. It's her favorite story—

Lava Man.

Lava Man? Herakles grinned at Geryon as they shot onto the freeway.

You're going to love my family.

XII. LAVA

He did not know how long he had been asleep.

––––––––

Black central stalled night. He lay hot and motionless, that is, motion

was a memory he could not recover

(among others) from the bottom of the vast blind kitchen where he was buried.

He could feel the house of sleepers

around him like loaves on shelves. There was a steady rushing sound

perhaps an electric fan down the hall

and a fragment of human voice tore itself out and came past, it seemed

already long ago, trailing

a bad dust of its dream which touched his skin. He thought of women.

What is it like to be a woman

listening in the dark? Black mantle of silence stretches between them

like geothermal pressure.

Ascent of the rapist up the stairs seems as slow as lava. She listens

to the blank space where

his consciousness is, moving towards her. Lava can move as slow as

nine hours per inch.

Color and fluidity vary with its temperature from dark red and hard

(below 1,800 degrees centigrade)

to brilliant yellow and completely fluid (above 1,950 degrees centigrade).

She wonders if

he is listening too. The cruel thing is, she falls asleep listening.

XIII. SOMNAMBULA

Geryon awoke too fast and felt his box contract.

———

Hot pressure morning. Houseful of tumbling humans and their languages.
Where am I?
Voices from somewhere. He made his way thickly downstairs
and through the house
to the back porch, huge and shadowy as a stage facing onto brilliant day.
Geryon squinted.
Grass swam towards him and away. Joyous small companies of insects
with double-decker wings
like fighter planes were diving about in the hot white wind. The light
unbalanced him,
he sat down quickly on the top step. Saw Herakles stretched on the grass
making sleepy talk.
My world is very slow right now, Herakles was saying. His grandmother
sat at the picnic table
eating toast and discussing death. She told of her brother who was conscious
to the end but could not speak.
His eyes watched the tubes they were putting in and pulling out of him so
they explained each one.
Now we are inserting sap of the queen of the night you will feel a pinch
then a black flow, said Herakles
in his sleepy voice that no one was listening to. A big red butterfly
went past riding on a little black one.
How nice, said Geryon, *he's helping him.* Herakles opened one eye and looked.

///////

He's fucking him.

Herakles! said his grandmother. He closed his eyes.

My heart aches when I am bad.

Then he looked at Geryon and smiled. *Can I show you our volcano?*

XIV. RED PATIENCE

Geryon did not know why he found the photograph disturbing.

———

She had taken it herself standing on the roof of the house that afternoon in 1923
with a box camera. "Red Patience."
A fifteen-minute exposure that recorded both the general shape of the cone
with its surroundings (best seen by day)
and the rain of incandescent bombs tossed into the air and rolling down its slopes
(visible in the dark).
Bombs had shot through the vent at velocities of more than three hundred kilometers
an hour, she told him. The cone itself
rose a thousand meters above the original cornfield and erupted about a million tons
of ash, cinder, and bombs during its early months.
Lava followed for twenty-nine months. Across the bottom of the photograph
Geryon could see a row of pine skeletons
killed by falling ash. "Red Patience." A photograph that has compressed
on its motionless surface
fifteen different moments of time, nine hundred seconds of bombs moving up
and ash moving down
and pines in the kill process. Geryon did not know why
he kept going back to it.
It was not that he found it an especially pleasing photograph.
It was not that he
did not understand how such photographs are made.
He kept going back to it.

What if you took a fifteen-minute exposure of a man in jail, let's say the lava

has just reached his window?

he asked. *I think you are confusing subject and object,* she said.

Very likely, said Geryon.

XV. PAIR

These days Geryon was experiencing a pain not felt since childhood.

————

His wings were struggling. They tore against each other on his shoulders
like the little mindless red animals they were.
With a piece of wooden plank he'd found in the basement Geryon made a back brace
and lashed the wings tight.
Then put his jacket back on. *You seem moody today Geryon anything wrong?*
said Herakles when he saw Geryon
coming up the basement stairs. His voice had an edge. He liked to see Geryon happy.
Geryon felt his wings turn in, and in, and in.
Nope just fine. Geryon smiled hard with half of his face. *So tomorrow Geryon.*
Tomorrow?
Tomorrow we'll take the car and drive out to the volcano you'll like that.
Yes.
Get some photographs. Geryon sat down suddenly. *And tonight—Geryon? You okay?*
Yes fine, I'm listening. Tonight—?
Why do you have your jacket over your head?

. . . .

Can't hear you Geryon. The jacket shifted. Geryon peered out. *I said sometimes*
I need a little privacy.
Herakles was watching him, his eyes still as a pond. They watched each other,
this odd pair.

XVI. GROOMING

As in childhood we live sweeping close to the sky and now, what dawn is this.

———

Herakles lies like a piece of torn silk in the heat of the blue saying,

Geryon please. The break in his voice

made Geryon think for some reason of going into a barn

first thing in the morning

when sunlight strikes a bale of raw hay still wet from the night.

Put your mouth on it Geryon please.

Geryon did. It tasted sweet enough. I am learning a lot in this year of my life,

thought Geryon. It tasted very young.

Geryon felt clear and powerful—not some wounded angel after all

but a magnetic person like Matisse

or Charlie Parker! Afterwards they lay kissing for a long time then

played gorillas. Got hungry.

Soon they were sitting in a booth at the Bus Depot waiting for food.

They had started to practice

their song ("Joy to the World") when Herakles pulled Geryon's head

into his lap and began grooming

for nits. Gorilla grunts mingled with breakfast sounds in the busy room.

The waitress arrived

holding two plates of eggs. Geryon gazed up at her from under Herakles' arm.

Newlyweds? she said.

XVII. WALLS

That night they went out painting.

———

Geryon did an early red-winged LOVESLAVE on the garage of the priest's house

next to the Catholic church.

Then passing down Main Street they saw fat white letters (recent) on the side

of the post office. CAPITALISM SUCKS.

Herakles eyed the paint supply dubiously. *Well.* He parked in the alley.

After crossing out the white letters

neatly with a bar of opaque black he encircled it in an airy red cloud

of chancery script.

CUT HERE. He was quiet as they got back into the car.

Then down the tunnel

to the on-ramp for the freeway. Geryon was bored and said he couldn't see any

good spaces left,

got out his camera and went off towards the sound of traffic. Up on the overpass

the night was wide open

and blowing headlights like a sea. He stood against the wind and let it peel him

clean.

Back at the tunnel Herakles had finished printing his seven personal precepts

in vertical black and red over a fading

stenciled LEAVE THE WALLS ALONE and was down on one knee scraping

the brush on the edge of the can.

He did not look up but said, *There's some paint left—another LOVESLAVE?—no*

let's do something cheerful.

All your designs are about captivity, it depresses me.

Geryon watched the top of Herakles' head

and felt his limits returning. Nothing to say. Nothing. He looked at this fact

in mild surprise. Once in childhood

his ice cream had been eaten by a dog. Just an empty cone

in a small dramatic red fist.

Herakles stood up. *No? Let's go then.* On the way home they tried "Joy to the World"

but were too tired. It seemed a long drive.

XVIII. SHE

Back at the house all was dark except a light from the porch.

———————

Herakles went to see. Geryon had a thought to call home and ran upstairs.
You can use the phone in my mother's room

top of the stairs turn left, Herakles called after him. But when he reached the room
he stopped in a night gone suddenly solid.

Who am I? He had been here before in the dark on the stairs with his hands out
groping for a switch—he hit it

and the room sprang towards him like an angry surf with its unappeasable debris
of woman liquors, he saw a slip

a dropped magazine combs baby powder a stack of phone books a bowl of pearls
a teacup with water in it himself

in the mirror cruel as a slash of lipstick—he banged the light off.

He had been here before, dangling

inside the word *she* like a trinket at a belt. Spokes of red rang across his eyelids
in the blackness.

As he made his way downstairs again Geryon could hear the grandmother's voice.
She was sitting in the porch swing

with her hands in her lap and her small feet dangling. A rectangle of light
fell across the porch from the kitchen door

and just touched her hem. Herakles lay flat on his back on top of the picnic table,
both arms across his face.

The grandmother watched Geryon cross the porch and sit down between them
in a deck chair

without interrupting her sentence—*this idea that your lungs will explode*

- - - - - - - - -

57

if you can't reach the surface—

lungs don't explode they collapse without oxygen I have it from Virginia Woolf

who once spoke to me at a party not of course

about drowning of which she had no idea yet—have I told you this story before?

I remember the sky behind her was purple she

came towards me saying Why are you alone in this huge blank garden

like a piece of electricity? *Electricity?*

Maybe she said cakes and tea true we were drinking gin it was long past

teatime but she was a highly original woman

I was praying God let it have been cakes and tea I'll tell her my anecdote

of Buenos Aires those Argentines

so crazy for tea every day at five the little cups but she drifted away the little

translucent cups like bones you know

in Buenos Aires I had a small dog but I see by your face I am wandering.

Geryon jumped. *No ma'am*, he yelled

as the deck chair gouged him. *Gift from Freud but that is another story.*

Yes ma'am?

He drowned not Freud the dog and Freud made a joke it was not a funny joke

having to do with incomplete transference I cannot

recall the German wording the German weather however I remember exactly.

What was the weather ma'am?

Cold and moonlit. You met with Freud at night? Only in summer.

The phone rang and Herakles

fell off the table then ran to answer it. July moonshadows stood motionless

on the grass. Geryon watched

a presence soaking out of them. *What was I saying? Oh yes Freud reality*

is a web Freud used to say—

Ma'am? Yes. Can I ask you something? Certainly. I want to know about Lava Man.
Ah.

I want to know what he was like. He was badly burned. But he didn't die?
Not in the jail.

And then what? And then he joined with Barnum you know the Barnum Circus
he toured United States made a lot

of money I saw the show in Mexico City when I was twelve. Was it a good show?
Pretty good Freud would have called it

unconscious metaphysics but at twelve I was not cynical I had a good time.
So what did he do? He gave out

souvenir pumice and showed where the incandescence had brushed him
I am a drop of gold he would say

I am molten matter returned from the core of earth to tell you interior things—
Look! he would prick his thumb

and press out ocher-colored drops that sizzled when they hit the plate—
Volcano blood! Claimed

the temperature of his body was a continuous 130 degrees and let people
touch his skin for 75 cents

at the back of the tent. So you touched him? She paused. *Let's say—*
Herakles bounded in.

It's your mom. She's finished yelling at me now she wants to talk to you.

XIX. FROM THE ARCHAIC
TO
THE FAST SELF

Reality is a sound, you have to tune in to it not just keep yelling.

———

He woke fast from a loud wild dream that vanished at once and lay listening
to the splendid subtle ravines of Hades
where hardworking dawn monkeys were wheedling and baiting one another
up and down the mahogany trees.
The cries took little nicks out of him. This was when Geryon liked to plan
his autobiography, in that blurred state
between awake and asleep when too many intake valves are open in the soul.
Like the terrestrial crust of the earth
which is proportionately ten times thinner than an eggshell, the skin of the soul
is a miracle of mutual pressures.
Millions of kilograms of force pounding up from earth's core on the inside to meet
the cold air of the world and stop,
as we do, just in time. The autobiography,
which Geryon worked on from the age of five to the age of forty-four,
had recently taken the form
of a photographic essay. Now that I am a man in transition, thought Geryon
using a phrase he'd learned from—
door hit the wall as Herakles kicked it open and entered carrying a tray
with two cups and three bananas.
Room service, said Herakles looking around for a place to set the tray down.
Geryon had moved all the furniture

up against the walls of the room. *Oh good,* said Geryon. *Coffee.*

No it's tea, said Herakles.

My grandmother is in Argentina again today. He handed Geryon a banana.
She was just telling me about the electricians.
You know you have to pass an examination to get into the electricians' union
in Buenos Aires but all the exam questions
are about the constitution. What do you mean the human constitution?
No the constitution of Argentina
except the last one. The last constitution? No the last question on the exam—
guess what it is you'll never guess. Guess.
No.

Come on. No I hate guessing. Just one guess come on Geryon just one.
What time of day did Krakatoa erupt?
Great question but no. He paused. *Give up?* Geryon looked at him.
What is the Holy Ghost?
That's it? That's it. What is the Holy Ghost—a truly electrical question!
as my grandmother put it.

Herakles was sitting on the floor beside the bed. He drained his teacup
and regarded Geryon.

So what time of day did Krakatoa erupt? Four a.m., Geryon said pulling the quilt
high up under his chin.

The noise awakened sleepers in Australia three thousand kilometers away.
No kidding how do you know that?

Geryon had found the *Encyclopaedia Britannica* (1911 edition) in the basement
and read the Volcano article.

Should he admit this? Yes. *Encyclopedia.* Herakles peeled a banana.
He seemed to be thinking.

So your mom was pretty angry last night. Geryon said *Yes.* Herakles ate
half his banana. He ate the other half.
So what do you think? What do you mean what do I think? Herakles placed
his banana peel on the tray
and straightened the parts of it carefully. *Think you should be getting back?*
Geryon was chewing
a mouthful of banana and didn't quite hear. This sentence is important for you,
said a little lulled voice inside.
What? I said there's a bus every morning at nine or so. Geryon was trying
to breathe but a red wall
had sliced the air in half. *And what about you? Oh I'll be staying around here
I guess my grandmother wants
the house painted said she'd pay me I can probably get a couple guys
from town to help.*
Geryon was thinking hard. Flames licked along the floorboards inside him.
I am quite a good painter myself, he said.
But the word *good* cracked in half. Herakles watched him. *Geryon you know
we'll always be friends.*
Geryon's heart and lungs were a black crust. He had a sudden strong desire
to go to sleep. Herakles slid to his feet
smooth as a monkey. *Hurry up and get dressed Geryon we're going to show you
a volcano today I'll be
on the porch my grandmother wants to come too.*
In Geryon's autobiography
this page has a photograph of some red rabbit giggle tied with a white ribbon.
He has titled it "Jealous of My Little Sensations."

XX. AA

Geryon fell asleep seven or eight times on the way to the volcano.

———

The other two were talking about feminism then life in Hades then unstable bitumen

or was that from *Britannica?* All

the sentences mixed around in Geryon's drifting drowsing head *men*

had to be taught

to hate women for foot massage pumice and ballast on railroad sure

they know how eruption

takes place his little elementary courtesies darting out like a tongue but

how can I talk

to people who don't know the European experience—now

jolted awake Geryon

glanced out. The world had gone black and bulbous. Shiny ropes of old lava

rose and fell in every direction

around the car which had come to a halt. Most volcanic rock is basalt.

If it is dark and blocky that means

very little silica in the composition (so the *Encyclopaedia Britannica*).

Very little silica in the composition,

said Geryon as he climbed out. Then the rock silenced him.

It pitched away on all sides

utterly blank except for one crazed blackish unit of intraplate light

bouncing from rock to rock

as if looking for lost kin. Geryon put his foot out to take a step.

The lava emitted

a glassy squeak and he jumped. *Careful,* said Herakles' grandmother.

Herakles had lifted her out of the back seat,

now she stood leaning on his arm. *The lava dome here is more than ninety percent*

glass—rhyolite obsidian they call it. I find

it very beautiful. Has a kind of pulse as you look at it. She began to move

forward with a tinkling sound

over the black billows. *They say the reason for all these blocks and rubble on top*

is strains produced when the glass

chills so rapidly. She made a little sound. *Reminds me of my marriage.* She

stumbled then and Geryon

caught her other arm, it was like a handful of autumn. He felt huge and wrong.

When is it polite to let go someone's arm

after you grab it?

Just for an instant balancing on the vitreous surface he went to sleep and awoke

still gripping her arm, Herakles was saying

. . . in crossword puzzles. It's the word for blocky lava in Hawaiian.

How do you spell it?

Just like it sounds—aa. Geryon dozed off, awoke again, they were in the car

already driving away

from the terrible rocks. Up front Herakles and his grandmother had begun

"Joy to the World" in harmony.

XXI. MEMORY BURN

Herakles and Geryon had gone to the video store.

———

Full moon sends rapid clouds dashing past a cold sky. When they came back
they were arguing.
It's not the photograph that disturbs you it's you don't understand what photography is.
Photography is disturbing, said Geryon.
Photography is a way of playing with perceptual relationships.
Well exactly.
But you don't need a camera to tell you that. What about stars?
Are you going to tell me
none of the stars are really there? Well some are there but some burned out
ten thousand years ago.
I don't believe that.
How can you not believe it, it's a known fact. But I see them. You see memories.
Have we had this conversation before?
Geryon followed Herakles to the back porch. They sat on opposite ends of the sofa.
Do you know how far away some of those stars are?
Just don't believe it. Let's see someone touch a star and not get burned. He'll
hold up his finger, Just a memory burn! he'll say
then I'll believe it. Okay never mind stars what about sound, you've watched
a man chop wood in a forest.
No I do not watch men in forests.
I give up. That would be very cold. What? That would be very cold, repeated
the grandmother from the porch swing.
Watching men in forests? A memory burn. Ah. She's right. Yes she is she

had lung burn once

and that was cold and don't call me she when I'm right here.

Sorry.

You got lung burn in Hades? No it was in the Pyrenees I burned my lungs I had

gone to St. Croix to photograph skiers

that would be the winter Olympics 1936 Grushenk was competing do you know

Grushenk? Well never mind he was very fast

I sold a photograph of him in his extraordinary scarlet ski pants

to Life *magazine for a thousand dollars.*

That was a handsome sum in 1936. Don't be patronizing it's still a handsome sum—

for a photograph. Herakles' father

(she waved her hand towards the sofa but Herakles had gone back in the house)

gave me less than half that for "Red Patience"—

you took a look at "Red Patience" didn't you? I wish he hadn't hung it in the kitchen

much too dark in there

people think it's a black-and-white photograph of course nobody knows

how to look at a photograph nowadays.

No I saw the lava, is it lava? Of course yes you mean at the top of the cone.

No I mean at the bottom

of the picture on the trunk of one of the pine trees little red drops like blood.

Ah yes very good the little red drops

my signature. It is a disturbing photograph. Yes. But why?

"Gaiety transfiguring all that dread."

Who said that? Yeats.

Where did Yeats see a volcano? I believe he was talking about politics. No

I don't think that's what I mean.

Do you mean the silence. But all photographs are silent. Don't be facile you might as well say all mothers

are women. Well aren't they? Of course but that tells you nothing. Question is

how they use it—given

the limits of the form— Does your mother live on the island? I don't want

to talk about my mother.

Ah well. Silence then. Herakles came out the door from the kitchen.

Climbed over the back of the sofa

and subsided into it lengthwise. *Your grandmother has been teaching me*

the value of silence, said Geryon.

I bet, said Herakles. He turned to her. *It's late Gram don't you want to go to bed?*

Can't sleep angel, she said.

Is your leg paining? I can rub your ankles. Come I'll take you up.

Herakles was standing in front of her

and he lifted her towards him like snow. Geryon saw her legs were asymmetrical,

one pointed up the other down and back.

Goodnight children, she called in her voice like old coals.

May God favor you with dreams.

XXII. FRUIT BOWL

His mother was sitting at the kitchen table when Geryon opened the screen door.

————

He had taken the local bus from Hades. Seven-hour trip. He wept most of the way.

Wanted to go straight to his room

and shut the door but when he saw her he sat down. Hands in his jacket.

She smoked in silence a moment

then rested her chin against her hand. Eyes on his chest. *Nice T-shirt,* she said.

It was a red singlet with white letters

that read TENDER

      LOIN. *Herakles gave it—*and here Geryon had meant

to slide past the name coolly

but such a cloud of agony poured up his soul he couldn't remember

what he was saying.

He sat forward. She exhaled. She was watching his hands so he unclenched them

from the edge

of the table and began spinning the fruit bowl slowly. He spun it clockwise.

Counterclockwise. Clockwise.

Why is this fruit bowl always here? He stopped and held it by the rims.

It's always here and it never

has any fruit in it. Been here all my life never had fruit in it yet. Doesn't

that bother you? How do we even

know it's a fruit bowl? She regarded him through smoke. *How do you think it feels*

growing up in a house full

of empty fruit bowls? His voice was high. His eyes met hers and they began

to laugh. They laughed

until tears ran down. Then they sat quiet. Drifted back

to opposite walls.

They spoke of a number of things, laundry, Geryon's brother doing drugs,

the light in the bathroom.

At one point she took out a cigarette, looked at it, put it back. Geryon laid

his head on his arms on the table.

He was very sleepy. finally they rose and went their ways. The fruit bowl

stayed there. Yes empty.

XXIII. WATER

Water! Out from between two crouching masses of the world the word leapt.

———

It was raining on his face. He forgot for a moment that he was a brokenheart

then he remembered. Sick lurch

downward to Geryon trapped in his own bad apple. Each morning a shock

to return to the cut soul.

Pulling himself onto the edge of the bed he stared at the dull amplitude of rain.

Buckets of water sloshed from sky

to roof to eave to windowsill. He watched it hit his feet and puddle on the floor.

He could hear bits of human voice

streaming down the drainpipe—*I believe in being gracious*—

He slammed the window shut.

Below in the living room everything was motionless. Drapes closed, chairs asleep.

Huge wads of silence stuffed the air.

He was staring around for the dog then realized they hadn't had a dog for years. Clock

in the kitchen said quarter to six.

He stood looking at it, willing himself not to blink until the big hand bumped over

to the next minute. Years passed

as his eyes ran water and a thousand ideas jumped his brain—*If the world*

ends now I am free and

If the world ends now no one will see my autobiography—finally it bumped.

He had a flash of Herakles' sleeping house

and put that away. Got out the coffee can, turned on the tap and started to cry.

Outside the natural world was enjoying

a moment of total strength. Wind rushed over the ground like a sea and battered up into the corners of the buildings,

garbage cans went dashing down the alley after their souls.

Giant ribs of rain shifted

open on a flash of light and cracked together again, making the kitchen clock

bump crazily. Somewhere a door slammed.

Leaves tore past the window. Weak as a fly Geryon crouched against the sink

with his fist in his mouth

and his wings trailing over the drainboard. Rain lashing the kitchen window

sent another phrase

of Herakles' chasing across his mind. *A photograph is just a bunch of light*

hitting a plate. Geryon wiped his face

with his wings and went out to the living room to look for the camera.

When he stepped onto the back porch

rain was funnelling down off the roof in a morning as dark as night.

He had the camera wrapped

in a sweatshirt. The photograph is titled "If He Sleep He Shall Do Well."

It shows a fly floating in a pail of water—

drowned but with a strange agitation of light around the wings. Geryon used

a fifteen-minute exposure.

When he first opened the shutter the fly seemed to be still alive.

XXIV. FREEDOM

Geryon's life entered a numb time, caught between the tongue and the taste.

———

He got a job in the local library shelving government documents. It was
agreeable to work in a basement
humming with fluorescent tubes and cold as a sea of stone. The documents
had a forlorn austerity,
tall and hushed in their ranges as veterans of a forgotten war. Whenever
a librarian came clumping
down the metal stairs with a pink slip for one of the documents,
Geryon would vanish into the stacks.
A little button at the end of each range activated the fluorescent track above it.
A yellowing 5 × 7 index card
Scotch-taped below each button said EXTINGUISH LIGHT WHEN NOT IN USE.
Geryon went flickering
through the ranges like a bit of mercury flipping the switches on and off.
The librarians thought him
a talented boy with a shadow side. One evening at supper when his mother
asked him
what they were like, Geryon could not remember if the librarians were men
or women. He had taken a number
of careful photographs but these showed only the shoes and socks of each person.
They look like mostly men's shoes to me,
said his mother bending over the prints which he had spread on the kitchen table.
Except—who's that? she pointed.
It was a photograph taken from floor level of a single naked foot propped on
the open drawer of a metal file cabinet.

- - - - - - -

On the floor beneath lay a dirty red Converse sneaker on its side.

That's the assistant head librarian's sister.

He pulled forward a photo of white acrylic socks and dark loafers

crossed at the ankle: assistant head librarian.

She comes in at five sometimes to get a ride home with him. Geryon's mother

looked closer. *What does she do?*

Works at Dunkin' Donuts I think. Nice girl? No. Yes. I don't know.

Geryon glared. His mother reached out

a hand to touch his head but he ducked sideways and began gathering up

the photographs. The phone rang.

Can you get that? she said turning to the sink. Geryon went into the living room

and stood looking down at the phone

as it rang a third time and a fourth. *Hello? Geryon? Hi it's me. You sound*

funny were you asleep?

Herakles' voice went bouncing through Geryon on hot gold springs.

Oh. No. No I wasn't.

So how are things? What are you up to? Oh— Geryon sat down hard on the rug.

fire was closing off his lungs—

not much. You? Oh the usual you know this and that did some good painting

last night with Hart. Heart?

I guess you didn't meet Hart when you were here he came over from

the mainland last Saturday

or was it Friday no Saturday Hart is a boxer says he might train me to be

his corner man. Really.

A good corner man can make the difference Hart says.

Does he.

Muhammad Ali had a corner man named Mr. Kopps they used to hunch down

there on the rope and write poems

///////
73

together in between rounds. Poems. But that's not why I called Geryon

the reason I called is to tell you

about my dream I had a dream of you last night. Did you. Yes you were this

old Indian guy standing on the back porch

and there was a pail of water there on the step with a drowned bird in it—

big yellow bird really huge you know

floating with its wings out and you leaned over and said, Come on now

get out of there—*and you took it*

by one wing and just flung it right up into the air WHOOSH *it came alive*

and then it was gone.

Yellow? said Geryon and he was thinking Yellow! Yellow! Even in dreams

he doesn't know me at all! Yellow!

What'd you say Geryon?

Nothing.

It's a freedom dream Geryon.

Yes.

Freedom is what I want for you Geryon we're true friends you know that's why

I want you to be free.

Don't want to be free want to be with you. Beaten but alert Geryon organized all

his inside force to suppress this remark.

Guess I better get off the line now Geryon my grandmother gets mad

if I run up her bill but it's real nice

to hear your voice. . . . .

Geryon? All right if I use the phone now? I have to call Maria. His mother

standing in the doorway.

Oh yes sure. Geryon replaced the receiver. *Sorry. You okay? Yes.* He tilted

to his feet. *Going out.*

74

Where? she said as he angled past her in the doorway.

Beach.

Won't you need a jacket— The screen door slammed. It was

well past midnight

when Geryon got back. The house was dark. He climbed to his room.

After undressing he stood

at the mirror and observed himself emptily. Freedom! The chubby knees

the funny red smell the saddening ways.

He sank onto the bed and lay full length. Tears ran back into his ears awhile

then no more tears.

He had touched bottom. Feeling bruised but pure he switched off the light.

Fell instantly asleep.

Anger slammed the red fool awake at three a.m. he kept trying to breathe each time

he lifted his head it pounded him

again like a piece of weed against a hard black beach. Geryon sat up suddenly.

The sheet was drenched.

He switched on the light. He was staring at the sweep hand of the electric clock

on the dresser. Its little dry hum

ran over his nerves like a comb. He forced his eyes away. The bedroom doorway

gaped at him black as a keyhole.

His brain was jerking forward like a bad slide projector. He saw the doorway

the house the night the world and

on the other side of the world somewhere Herakles laughing drinking getting

into a car and Geryon's

whole body formed one arch of a cry—upcast to that custom, the human custom

of wrong love.

XXV. TUNNEL

Geryon was packing when the phone rang.

———

He knew who it was even though, now that he was twenty-two and lived
on the mainland, he spoke to her
usually on Saturday mornings. He climbed across his suitcase and reached
for the phone, knocking
the *Fodor's Guide to South America* and six boxes of DX 100 color film into the sink.
Small room.

Hi Mom yes just about

. . . .

No I got a window seat

. . . .

Seventeen but there's a three-hour difference between here and Buenos Aires

. . . .

No listen I phoned—

. . . .

I phoned the consulate today there are no shots required for Argentina

. . . .

Mom be reasonable Flying Down to Rio *was made in 1933 and it's set in Brazil*

. . . .

Like when we went to Florida and Dad swelled up

. . . .

Yes okay

. . . .

Well you know what the gauchos say

. . . .

Something about riding boldly into nullity

. . . .

Not exactly it feels like a tunnel

. . . .

*Okay I'll call as soon as I get to the hotel—Mom? I have to go now the taxi's
here listen don't smoke too much*

. . . .

Me too

. . . .

Bye

XXVI. AEROPLANE

It is always winter up there.

———————

As the aeroplane moved over the frozen white flatland of the clouds Geryon left
his life behind like a weak season.
Once he'd seen a dog having a rabies attack. Springing about like a mechanical toy
and falling over on its back
in jerky ways as if worked by wires. When the owner stepped up and put a gun
to the dog's temple Geryon walked away.
Now leaning forward to peer out the little oblong window where icy cloudlight
drilled his eyes
he wished he had stayed to see it go free.
Geryon was hungry.
Opening his *Fodor's Guide* he began to read "Things to Know About Argentina."
"The strongest harpoons are made
from the bone inside the skull of a whale that beaches on Tierra del Fuego.
Inside the skull is a *canalita*
and along it two bones. Harpoons made from a jawbone are not so strong."
A delicious odor of roasting seal
was wafting through the aeroplane. He looked up. Rows away at the front
servants were distributing
dinner from a cart. Geryon was very hungry. He forced himself to stare out
the cold little window and count
to one hundred before looking up again. The cart had not moved. He thought
about harpoons. Does a man with a harpoon
go hungry? Even a harpoon made of a jawbone could hit the cart from here.

How people get power over one another,

this mystery. He moved his eyes back to the *Fodor's Guide.* "Among

the indigenous folk of Tierra del Fuego

were the Yamana which means as a noun 'people not animals' or as a verb

'to live, breathe, be happy, recover

from sickness, become sane.' Joined as a suffix to the word for *hand*

it denotes 'friendship.' "

Geryon's dinner arrived. He unwrapped and ate every item ravenously seeking

the smell he had smelled

a few moments ago but it was not there. The Yamana too, he read, were extinct

by the beginning of the twentieth century—

wiped out by measles contracted from the children of English missionaries.

As night darkness glided across the outer world

the inside of the aeroplane got colder and smaller. There were neon tracks

in the ceiling which extinguished themselves.

Geryon closed his eyes and listened to engines vibrating deep in the moon-splashed

canals of his brain. Each way

he moved brought his kneecaps into hard contact with punishment.

He opened his eyes again.

At the very front of the cabin hung a video screen. South America glowed

like an avocado. A live red line

marked the progress of the aeroplane. He watched the red line inch forward

from Miami

towards Puerto Rico at 972 kilometers per hour. The passenger in front of him

had propped his video camera

gently against the sleeping head of his wife and was videotaping the video screen,

which now recorded

Temperatura Exterior (−50 degrees C) and Altura (10,670 meters)
as well as Velocidad.
"The Yamana, whose filth and poverty persuaded Darwin, passing in his *Beagle,*
that they were monkey men unworthy
of study, had fifteen names for clouds and more than fifty for different kinds
of kin. Among their variations of the verb
'to bite' was a word that meant 'to come surprisingly on a hard substance
when eating something soft
e.g. a pearl in a mussel.' " Geryon shifted himself down and up in the molded
seat trying to unclench
knots of pain in his spine. Half turned sideways but could not place his left arm.
Heaved himself forwards again
accidentally punching off the reading light and knocking his book to the floor.
The woman next to him moaned
and slumped over the armrest like a wounded seal. He sat in the numb dark.
Hungry again.
The video screen recorded local (Bermuda) time as ten minutes to two.
What is time made of?
He could feel it massed around him, he could see its big deadweight blocks
padded tight together
all the way from Bermuda to Buenos Aires—too tight. His lungs contracted.
Fear of time came at him. Time
was squeezing Geryon like the pleats of an accordion. He ducked his head to peer
into the little cold black glare of the window.
Outside a bitten moon rode fast over a tableland of snow. Staring at the vast black
and silver nonworld moving
and not moving incomprehensibly past this dangling fragment of humans

⁄ ⁄ ⁄ ⁄ ⁄ ⁄ ⁄ ⁄

80

he felt its indifference roar over

his brain box. An idea glazed along the edge of the box and whipped back

down into the canal behind the wings

and it was gone. A man moves through time. It means nothing except that,

like a harpoon, once thrown he will arrive.

Geryon leaned his forehead against the cold hard hum of the double glass and slept.

On the floor under his feet

Fodor's Guide lay open. THE GAUCHO ACQUIRED AN EXAGGERATED NOTION

OF MASTERY OVER

HIS OWN DESTINY FROM THE SIMPLE ACT OF RIDING ON HORSEBACK

WAY FAR ACROSS THE PLAIN.

XXVII. MITWELT

There is no person without a world.

————

The red monster sat at a corner table of Café Mitwelt writing bits of Heidegger
on the postcards he'd bought.

> *Sie sind das was betreiben*
> there are many Germans in
> Buenos Aires they are all
> soccer players the weather
> is lovely wish you were here
> GERYON

he wrote to his brother now a sportscaster at a radio station on the mainland.
Over at the end of the bar
near the whiskey bottles Geryon saw a waiter speaking to another behind his hand.
He supposed they would
soon throw him out. Could they tell from the angle of his body, from the way
his hand moved that he was
writing German not Spanish? It was likely illegal. Geryon had been studying
German philosophy at college
for the past three years, the waiters doubtless knew this too. He shifted his upper
back muscles inside
the huge overcoat, tightening his wings and turned over another postcard.

Zum verlorenen Hören

There are many Germans

in Buenos Aires they are

all psychoanalysts the

weather is lovely wish you

were here

     GERYON

he wrote to his philosophy professor. But now he noticed one of the waiters

coming towards him. A cold spray

of fear shot across his lungs. He rummaged inside himself for Spanish phrases.

Please do not call the police—

what did Spanish sound like? he could not recall a single word of it.

German irregular verbs

were marching across his mind as the waiter drew up at his table and stood,

a brilliant white towel

draped on his forearm, leaning slightly towards Geryon. *Aufwarts abwarts*

ruckwarts vorwarts auswarts einwarts

swam crazy circles around each other while Geryon watched the waiter extract

a coffee cup smoothly

from the debris of postcards covering the table and straighten his towel

as he asked in perfect English

Would the gentleman like another expresso? but Geryon was already blundering

to his feet with the postcards

in one hand, coins dropping on the tablecloth and he went crashing out.

It was not the fear of ridicule,

to which everyday life as a winged red person had accommodated Geryon early in life, but this blank desertion of his own mind

that threw him into despair. Perhaps he was mad. In the seventh grade he had done

a science project on this worry.

It was the year he began to wonder about the noise that colors make. Roses came

roaring across the garden at him.

He lay on his bed at night listening to the silver light of stars crashing against

the window screen. Most

of those he interviewed for the science project had to admit they did not hear

the cries of the roses

being burned alive in the noonday sun. *Like horses,* Geryon would say helpfully,

like horses in war. No, they shook their heads.

Why is grass called blades? he asked them. *Isn't it because of the clicking?*

They stared at him. *You should be*

interviewing roses not people, said the science teacher. Geryon liked this idea.

The last page of his project

was a photograph of his mother's rosebush under the kitchen window.

Four of the roses were on fire.

They stood up straight and pure on the stalk, gripping the dark like prophets

and howling colossal intimacies

from the back of their fused throats. *Didn't your mother mind—*

Signor! Something solid landed

against his back. Geryon had come to a dead halt in the middle of a sidewalk

in Buenos Aires

with people flooding around his big overcoat on every side. People, thought Geryon,

for whom life

is a marvelous adventure. He moved off into the tragicomedy of the crowd.

XXVIII. SKEPTICISM

A paste of blue cloud untangled itself on the red sky over the harbor.

———

Buenos Aires was blurring into dawn. Geryon had been walking for an hour

on the sweaty black cobblestones

of the city waiting for night's end. Traffic crashed past him. He covered his mouth

and nose with his hand as five old buses

came tilting around the corner of the street and halted one behind the other,

belching soot. Passengers streamed

on board like insects into lighted boxes and the experiment roared off down the street.

Pulling his body after him

like a soggy mattress Geryon trudged on uphill. Café Mitwelt was crowded.

He found a corner table

and was writing a postcard to his mother:

> *Die Angst offenbart das Nichts*
> There are many Germans in
> Buenos Aires they are all
> cigarette girls the weather
> is lov—

when he felt a sharp tap on his boot propped against the chair opposite.

Mind if I join you?

The yellowbeard had already taken hold of the chair. Geryon moved his boot.

Pretty busy in here today,

said the yellowbeard turning to signal a waiter—*Por favor hombre!*

Geryon went back to his postcard.

Sending postcards to your girlfriends? In the midst of his yellow beard

was a pink mouth small as a nipple. *No.*

You sound American am I right? You from the States?

No.

The waiter arrived with bread and jam to which the yellowbeard bent himself.

You here for the conference? No.

Big conference this weekend at the university. Philosophy. Skepticism.

Ancient or modern? Geryon

could not resist asking. *Well now,* said the yellowbeard looking up,

there's some ancient people here

and some modern people here. Flew me in from Irvine. My talk's at three.

What's your topic? said Geryon

trying not to stare at the nipple. *Emotionlessness.* The nipple puckered.

That is to say, what the ancients called

ataraxia. *Absence of disturbance,* said Geryon. *Precisely. You know ancient Greek?*

No but I have read the skeptics. So you

teach at Irvine. That's in California? Yes southern California—actually I've got

a grant next year to do research at MIT.

Geryon watched a small red tongue clean jam off the nipple. *I want to study the erotics*

of doubt. Why? Geryon asked.

The yellowbeard was pushing back his chair—*As a precondition*—and saluting

the waiters across the room—

of the proper search for truth. Provided you can renounce—he stood—*that*

rather fundamental human trait—

he raised both arms as if to alert a ship at sea—*the desire to know.* He sat.

I think I can, said Geryon.

Pardon? Nothing. A passing waiter slapped the bill down onto a small metal spike on the table.

Traffic was crashing past outside. Dawn had faded. The gas-white winter sky came down like a gag on Buenos Aires.

Would you care to come and hear my talk? We could share a cab.

May I bring my camera?

XXIX. SLOPES

Although a monster Geryon could be charming in company.

———————

He made an attempt as they hurtled across Buenos Aires in a small taxi.

The two of them

were crushed into the back seat with their knees against their chests,

Geryon unpleasantly aware

of the yellowbeard's thigh jolting against his own and of breath from the nipple.

He stared straight ahead.

The driver was out the window aiming a stream of rage at passing pedestrians

as the car shot across a red light.

He pounded the dashboard in joy and lit another cigarette, wheeling sharp left

to cut off a bicyclist

(who bounced onto the sidewalk and dove down a side street)

then veered diagonally in front

of three buses and halted shuddering behind another taxi. BLEEEEEEEEEEEEEEK.

Argentine horns sound like cows.

More blasphemy out the window. The yellowbeard was chuckling.

How's your Spanish? he said to Geryon.

Not very good what about you?

Actually I am fairly fluent. I spent a year in Spain doing research.

Emotionlessness?

No, law codes. I was looking at the sociology of ancient law codes.

You are interested in justice?

I'm interested in how people decide what sounds like a law.

So what's your favorite law code?

//////

Hammurabi. Why? Neatness. For example? For example:

"The man who is caught

stealing during a fire shall be thrown into the fire." Isn't that good?—if

there were such a thing

as justice that's what it ought to sound like—short. Clean. Rhythmical.

Like a houseboy.

Pardon? Nothing. They had arrived at the University of Buenos Aires.

The yellowbeard and the taxi driver

denounced one another for a few moments, then a pittance was paid over

and the taxi rattled off.

What is this place? said Geryon as they mounted the steps of a white concrete

warehouse covered with graffiti on the outside.

Inside it was colder than the winter air of the street. You could see your breath.

An abandoned cigarette factory, said the yellowbeard.

Why is it so cold?

They can't afford to heat it. The university's broke. The cavernous interior

was hung with banners.

Geryon photographed the yellowbeard beneath one that read

NIGHT ES SELBST ES

TALLER AUTOGESTIVO

JUEVES 18–21 HS

Then they made their way to a bare loft

called Faculty Lounge. No chairs. A long piece of brown paper nailed to the wall

had a list of names in pencil and pen.

Help Us Keep Track of Professors Detained or Disappeared, read the yellowbeard.

Muy impressivo, he said to a young man

standing nearby who merely looked at him. Geryon was trying to keep his eye

from resting on any one name.

Suppose it was the name of someone alive. In a room or in pain or waiting to die.

Once Geryon had gone

with his fourth-grade class to view a pair of beluga whales newly captured

from the upper rapids of the Churchill River.

Afterwards at night he would lie on his bed with his eyes open thinking of

the whales afloat

in the moonless tank where their tails touched the wall—as alive as he was

on their side

of the terrible slopes of time. *What is time made of?* Geryon said suddenly

turning to the yellowbeard who

looked at him surprised. *Time isn't made of anything. It is an abstraction.*

Just a meaning that we

impose upon motion. But I see—he looked down at his watch—*what you mean.*

Wouldn't want to be late

for my own lecture would I? Let's go.

Sunset begins early in winter, a bluntness at the edge of the light. Geryon

hurried after the yellowbeard

through dimming corridors, past students huddled in conversation who stubbed

their cigarettes underfoot

and did not look at him, to a bare brick-walled classroom with a muddle of small desks.

Empty one at the back.

It was a tight fit in his big overcoat. He couldn't cross his knees. Presences hunched

darkly in the other desks.

Clouds of cigarette smoke moved above them, butts lay thick on the concrete floor.

Geryon disliked a room without rows.

His brain went running back and forth over the disorder of desks trying to see

straight lines. Each time finding

an odd number it jammed then restarted. Geryon tried to pay attention.

Un poco misterioso, the yellowbeard

was saying. From the ceiling glared seventeen neon tubes. *I see the terrifying*

spaces of the universe hemming me in. . . .

the yellowbeard quoted Pascal and then began to pile words up all around the terror

of Pascal until it could scarcely be seen—

Geryon paused in his listening and saw the slopes of time spin backwards and stop.

He was standing beside his mother

at the window on a late winter afternoon. It was the hour when snow goes blue

and streetlights come on and a hare may

pause on the tree line as still as a word in a book. In this hour he and his mother

accompanied each other. They did not

turn on the light but stood quiet and watched the night come washing up

towards them. Saw

it arrive, touch, move past them and it was gone. Her ash glowed in the dark.

By now the yellowbeard had moved

from Pascal to Leibniz and was chalking a formula on the blackboard:

$$[\text{NEC}] = \text{A}\}\text{B}$$

which he articulated using the sentence "If Fabian is white Tomás is just as white."

Why Leibniz should be concerned

with the relative pallor of Fabian and Tomás did not come clear to Geryon

although he willed himself

to attend to the flat voice. He noted the word *necesariamente* recurring four times

then five times then the examples

turned inside out and now Fabian and Tomás were challenging each other's negritude.
If Fabian is black Tomás is just as black.

So this is skepticism, thought Geryon. White is black. Black is white. Perhaps soon
I will get some new information about red.

But the examples dried away into *la consecuencia* which got louder and louder as
the yellowbeard strode up and down

his kingdom of seriousness bordered by strong words, maintaining belief
in man's original greatness—

or was he denying it? Geryon may have missed a negative adverb—and ended
with Aristotle who had

compared skeptic philosophers to vegetables and to monsters. So blank and
so bizarre would be

the human life that tried to live outside belief in belief. Thus Aristotle.
The lecture ended

to a murmur of *Muchas gracias* from the audience. Then someone asked a question
and the yellowbeard

began talking again. Everybody lit another cigarette and clenched down in the desks.
Geryon watched smoke swirl.

Outside the sun had set. The little barred window was black. Geryon sat wrapped
in himself. Would this day never end?

His eye traveled to the clock at the front of the room and he fell into the pool
of his favorite question.

XXX . DISTANCES

"What is time made of?" is a question that had long exercised Geryon.

———

Everywhere he went he asked people. Yesterday for example at the university.
Time is an abstraction—just a meaning
that we impose upon motion. Geryon is thinking this answer over as he kneels
beside the bathtub in his hotel room
stirring photographs back and forth in the developing solution. He picks out
one of the prints and pins it
to a clothesline strung between the television and the door. It is a photograph
of some people sitting at desks
in a classroom. The desks look too small for them—but Geryon is not interested
in human comfort. Much truer
is the time that strays into photographs and stops. High on the wall hangs a white
electric clock. It says five minutes to six.
At five minutes after six that evening the philosophers had adjourned the classroom
and made their way to a bar
down the street called Guerra Civil. The yellowbeard rode proudly at the front
like a gaucho leading his infernal band
over the pampas. The gaucho is master of his environment, thought Geryon
clutching his camera and keeping to the rear.
Bar Guerra Civil was a white stucco room with a monk's table down the middle.
When Geryon arrived the others were
already deep in talk. He slid into a chair across from a man
in round spectacles.
What will you have Lazer? said someone on the man's left.

⁄ ⁄ ⁄ ⁄ ⁄ ⁄ ⁄

Oh let's see the cappuccino is good here

I'll have a cappuccino please lots of cinnamon and—he pushed up his spectacles—

a plate of olives.

He glanced across the table. *Your name is Lazarus?* said Geryon.

No my name is Lazer. As in laser beam—but

do you wish to order something? Geryon glanced at the waiter. *Coffee please.*

Turned back to Lazer. *Unusual name.*

Not really. I am named for my grandfather. Eleazar is a fairly common Jewish

name. But my parents

were atheists so—he spread his hands—*a slight accommodation.* He smiled.

And you are an atheist too? said Geryon.

I am a skeptic. You doubt God? Well more to the point I credit God

with the good sense to doubt me.

What is mortality after all but divine doubt flashing over us? For an instant God

suspends assent and POOF*! we disappear.*

It happens to me frequently. You disappear? Yes and then come back.

Moments of death I call them. Have an olive,

he added as the waiter's arm flashed between them with a plate.

Thank you, said Geryon

and bit into an olive. The pimiento stung his mouth alive like sudden sunset.

He was very hungry and ate seven more,

fast. Smiling a bit Lazer watched him. Y*ou eat like my daughter. With a certain*

shall I say lucidity.

How old is your daughter? asked Geryon. *Four—not quite human. Or perhaps*

a little beyond human. It is

because of her I began to notice moments of death. Children make you see distances.

What do you mean "distances"?

Lazer paused and picked an olive from the plate. He spun it slowly on the toothpick.

///////

Well for example this morning

I was sitting at my desk at home looking out on the acacia trees that grow beside

the balcony beautiful trees very tall

and my daughter was there she likes to stand beside me and draw pictures while

I write in my journal. It

was very bright this morning unexpectedly clear like a summer day and I looked up

and saw a shadow of a bird go flashing

across the leaves of the acacia as if on a screen projected and it seemed to me that I

was standing on a hill. I have labored up

to the top of this hill, here I am it has taken about half my life to get here and on

the other side the hill slopes down.

Behind me somewhere if I turned around I could see my daughter beginning to climb

hand over hand like a little gold

animal in the morning sun. That is who we are. Creatures moving on a hill.

At different distances, said Geryon.

At distances always changing. We cannot help one another or even cry out—

what would I say to her,

"Don't climb so fast"? The waiter passed behind Lazer. He was moving at a tilt.

Black outside air tossed itself

hard against the windows. Lazer looked down at his watch. *I must go,* he said

and he was winding his yellow scarf

about his neck as he rose. Oh don't go, thought Geryon who felt himself starting

to slide off the surface of the room

like an olive off a plate. When the plate attained an angle of thirty degrees

he would vanish into his own blankness.

But then his glance caught Lazer's. *I have enjoyed our conversation,* said Lazer.

Yes, said Geryon. *Thank you.*

They touched hands. Lazer bowed slightly and turned and went out. A gust of night pushed its way in the door

and everyone inside wavered once like stalks in a field then resumed their talk.
Geryon subsided into his overcoat

letting the talk flow over him warm as a bath. He felt for the moment concrete
and indivisible. The philosophers

were joking about cigarettes and Spanish banks and Leibniz, then politics.
One man recounted how

the governor of Puerto Rico had recently proclaimed it an injustice to exclude
citizens from the democratic process

merely because they were insane. Apparatus for voting was transported
to the state asylum. Indeed

the insane proved to be serious and creative voters. Many improved the ballot
by writing in candidates

they trusted would help the country. Eisenhower, Mozart, and St. John of the Cross
were popular suggestions. Now

the yellowbeard spoke up with a story from Spain. Franco too had understood
the uses of madness.

He was in the habit of busing large groups of supporters to his rallies.
On one occasion the local madhouses

were emptied for this purpose. Next day the newspapers reported cheerfully:
SUBNORMALS BEHIND YOU ALL THE WAY FRANCO!

Geryon's cheekbones hurt from smiling. He drained his water glass and chewed
the bits of ice then reached

across for Lazer's glass. He was ravenous. Try not to think about food. No hope
of dinner till probably ten p.m.

Willed his attention back to the conversation which had wandered to tails.
It is not widely known,

the yellowbeard was saying, *that twelve percent of babies in the world are born*
with tails. Doctors suppress this news.
They cut off the tail so it won't scare the parents. I wonder what percentage
are born with wings, said Geryon
into the collar of his overcoat. They went on to discuss the nature of boredom
ending with a long joke about monks
and soup that Geryon could not follow although it was explained to him twice.
The punch line contained
a Spanish phrase meaning *bad milk* which caused the philosophers to lean
their heads on the table in helpless joy.
Jokes make them happy, thought Geryon watching. Then a miracle occurred
in the form of a plate of sandwiches.
Geryon took three and buried his mouth in a delicious block of white bread
filled with tomatoes and butter and salt.
He thought about how delicious it was, how he liked slippery foods, how
slipperiness can be of different kinds.
I am a philosopher of sandwiches, he decided. Things good on the inside.
He would like to discuss this with someone.
And for a moment the frailest leaves of life contained him in a widening happiness.
When he got back to the hotel room
he set up the camera on the windowsill and activated the timer, then positioned
himself on the bed.
It is a black-and-white photograph showing a naked young man in fetal position.
He has entitled it "No Tail!"
The fantastic fingerwork of his wings is outspread on the bed like a black lace
map of South America.

XXXI. TANGO

Under the seams runs the pain.

———————

Panic jumped down on Geryon at three a.m. He stood at the window of his hotel room.
Empty street below gave back nothing of itself.
Cars nested along the curb on their shadows. Buildings leaned back out of the street.
Little rackety wind went by.
Moon gone. Sky shut. Night had delved deep. Somewhere (he thought) beneath
this strip of sleeping pavement
the enormous solid globe is spinning on its way—pistons thumping, lava pouring
from shelf to shelf,
evidence and time lignifying into their traces. At what point does one say of a man
that he has become unreal?
He hugged his overcoat closer and tried to assemble in his mind Heidegger's
argument about the use of moods.
We would think ourselves continuous with the world if we did not have moods.
It is state-of-mind that discloses to us
(Heidegger claims) that we are beings who have been thrown into something else.
Something else than what?
Geryon leaned his hot forehead against the filthy windowpane and wept.
Something else than this hotel room
he heard himself say and moments later he was charging along the hollow gutters
of Avenida Bolívar. Traffic was sparse.
He moved past shuttered kiosks and blank windows. Streets got narrower, darker.
Sloping down.
He could see the harbor blackly glittering. Cobblestones grew slick. Smell of salt fish

and latrines furred the air.

Geryon turned his collar up and walked west. Dirty river slapped along beside him.

Three soldiers observed him from a porch.

There was a sound of dripping behind the dark air—a voice. Geryon looked around.

Down the quay he could see

a dim square of light like a café or a shop. But there were no cafés down here.

What kind of shop would be open at four a.m.?

A big man stepped straight out into Geryon's path and stood adjusting the towel

on his arm. *Tango?* he said

and stepped back with a sweeping bow. Over the door Geryon read *Caminito*

in white neon as he stumbled down

into the soggy black interior of what (he later realized) was the only authentic

tango bar left in Buenos Aires.

Through the gloom he saw very old concrete walls lined with bottles and a circle

of tiny round red kitchen tables.

A gnome in an apron was darting about among the tables delivering the same tall

orangeish drink to everyone

in a glass like a test tube. A low stage at the front of the room was lit by spotlight.

Three ancient musicians hunched there—

piano, guitar, accordion. None of them looked less than seventy years old,

the accordion player so frail

each time he swayed his shoulders around a corner of the melody Geryon feared

the accordion would crush him flat.

It gradually became clear that nothing could crush this man. Hardly glancing

at one another the three of them played

as one person, in a state of pure discovery. They tore clear and clicked and locked

and unlocked, they shot

their eyebrows up and down. They leaned together and wove apart, they rose
and cut away and stalked
one another and flew up in a cloud and sank back down on waves. Geryon could not
take his eyes off them
and was rather annoyed when a man, no it was a woman, parted a curtain
and came onto the stage.
She wore a tuxedo with black tie. Detached a microphone from somewhere inside
the spotlight and began to sing.
It was a typical tango song and she had the throat full of needles you need to sing it.
Tangos are terrible—
Your heart or my death!—and they all sound the same. Geryon clapped every time
the other people clapped then
a new song started then they all began to blur into a stream that ran
down over the dirt floor
and then he was asleep, burning, yearning, dreaming, streaming, asleep.
Awoke with his cheekbone scraping the wall.
Looked around dully. Musicians gone. Tables empty. No lights on. Tango woman
leaning over a glass while the gnome
swept around her feet with a broom. He was dozing off again when he saw her rise
and turn towards him.
He jolted awake. Pulled his body upright inside the overcoat and tried to organize
his arms casually on the front of his person.
There seemed to be too many of them. In fact there were three since he had,
as usual, woke up with an erection
and today had no pants on (for reasons he could not immediately recall) but there
wasn't time to worry about this,
she was drawing a chair up to the table. *Buen'día,* she said.

Hi, said Geryon.

You American? No. English? No. German? No. Spy? Yes. She smiled.

He watched her extract

a cigarette and light it. She didn't speak. Geryon had a bad thought. Suppose

she was waiting for him

to say something about the music. Should he lie? Bolt? Try to distract her?

Your singing— he began and stopped.

The woman glanced up. *Tango is not for everyone,* she said. Geryon did not hear.

The cold pressure of the concrete wall

against his back had tumbled him into a recollection. He was at a Saturday night

high school dance. Basketball nets cast

their stretchy shadows high up the walls of the gym. Hours of music had crashed

on his ears while he stood

at the wall with his back pressed against cold concrete. Jolts from the stage

threw lit strips of human limbs

across the dark. Heat bloomed. Black night sky weighed starlessly on the windows.

Geryon stood upright

within the rayon planes of his brother's sports jacket. Sweat and desire ran

down his body to pool

in the crotch and behind the knees. He had been standing against the wall

for three and a half hours in a casual pose.

His eyes ached from the effort of trying to see everything without looking at it.

Other boys stood beside him

on the wall. The petals of their colognes rose around them in a light terror.

Meanwhile music pounded

across hearts opening every valve to the desperate drama of being

a self in a song.

Well? said his brother when Geryon came through the kitchen at five past midnight.
How was it? Who did you dance with? Do any dope?
Geryon paused. His brother was layering mayonnaise, bologna, and mustard onto
six pieces of bread laid out
on the counter beside the sink. Overhead the kitchen light shone sulfurous.
The bologna looked purple.
Geryon's eyes were still bouncing with images from the gym. *Oh this time I decided*
to sort of just watch you know.
Geryon's voice was loud in the too-bright room. His brother looked at him quickly
then went on piling up sandwiches
into a tower. He cut the tower diagonally in half with a downthrust of the bread knife
and piled it all onto a plate.
There was one piece of bologna left in the plastic which he shoved into his mouth as he
picked up the plate
and headed for the stairs leading down to the TV room. *Jacket looks good on you,*
he said thickly as he passed.
Clint Eastwood movie on the late show bring me down a blanket when you come.
Geryon stood thoughtful for a moment.
Then he replaced the lids on the mayonnaise and the mustard and put them back
in the fridge. Threw the bologna wrapper
in the garbage. Took a sponge and wiped the crumbs carefully across the counter
into the sink and ran water
until they disappeared. From the stainless steel of the kettle a small red person
in a big jacket regarded him.
Shall we dance? he said to it—KRRAAK—Geryon came abruptly awake
to gritty daylight in a tango bar.
The gnome was slamming chairs upside down on the red tables. Geryon could not

for the moment recall who she was

this woman sitting across from him knocking her cigarette on the edge of the table

and saying *Tango is not for everyone.*

She looked around the vacant room. The gnome was sweeping cigarette butts into a

pile. Original daylight trickled

weakly through gaps in the stiff little red curtains that hung at the windows.

She watched it. He

was trying to remember a line of a poem. *Nacht steigt ans Ufer . . .*

What did you say? she asked.

Nothing. He was very tired. The woman smoked in silence. *Do you ever*

wonder about beluga whales?

Geryon asked. Her eyebrows were startling, like two ascending insects.

It is an endangered species?

No I mean in tanks in captivity just floating.

No—why?

What do they think about? Floating in there. All night.

Nothing.

That's impossible.

Why?

You can't be alive and think about nothing. You *can't but you're not a whale.*

Why should it be different?

Why should it be the same? But I look in their eyes and I see them thinking.

Nonsense. It is yourself you see—it's guilt.

Guilt? Why would I be guilty about whales? Not my fault they're in a tank.

Exactly. So why are you guilty—whose

tank are you in? Geryon was exasperated. *Was your father a psychoanalyst?*

She grinned. *No it's me who's the psychoanalyst.*

He stared. She was serious. *Don't look so shocked,* she said. *It pays the rent*
and it's not immoral—
well not entirely immoral. But what about your singing? Hah! She flicked ash
to the floor. *Make a living singing tango?*
How many people did you see here tonight? Geryon thought. *five or six,* he said.
That's right. Those same five or six
are here every night. Goes up to nine or ten on weekends—maybe, if there's
no soccer on TV. Sometimes we get
a party of politicians from Chile or tourists from the States. But it's a fact.
Tango is a fossil.
So is psychoanalysis, said Geryon.
She studied him a few moments then said slowly—but the gnome gave the piano
a shove against the wall
and Geryon almost missed it—*Who can a monster blame for being red?*
What? said Geryon starting forward.
I said looks like time for you to get home to bed, she repeated, and stood,
pocketing her cigarettes.
Do come again, she said as Geryon's big overcoat swept out the door but he
did not turn his head.

XXXII. KISS

A healthy volcano is an exercise in the uses of pressure.

———————

Geryon sat on his bed in the hotel room pondering the cracks and fissures

of his inner life. It may happen

that the exit of the volcanic vent is blocked by a plug of rock, forcing

molten matter sideways along

lateral fissures called fire lips by volcanologists. Yet Geryon did not want

to become one of those people

who think of nothing but their stores of pain. He bent over the book on his knees.

Philosophic Problems.

". . . I will never know how you see red and you will never know how I see it.

But this separation of consciousness

is recognized only after a failure of communication, and our first movement is

to believe in an undivided being between us. . . ."

As he read Geryon could feel something like tons of black magma boiling up

from the deeper regions of him.

He moved his eyes back to the beginning of the page and started again.

"To deny the existence of red

is to deny the existence of mystery. The soul which does so will one day go mad."

A church bell rang across the page

and the hour of six P.M. flowed through the hotel like a wave. Lamps snapped on

and white bedspreads sprang forward,

water rushed in the walls, the elevator crashed like a mastodon within its hollow cage.

I am not the one who is crazy here,

said Geryon closing the book. He put on his coat, belted it formally, and went out.

Out on the street it was Saturday night

in Buenos Aires. Shoals of brilliant young men parted and closed around him.

Heaps of romance spilled their bright vapor

onto the pavement from behind plate glass. He stopped to stare at the window

of a Chinese restaurant where

forty-four cans of lichee nuts were piled into a tower as big as himself. He tripped

over a beggar woman

low on the curb with two children pooled in her skirts. He

paused at a newspaper kiosk

and read every headline. Then went round the other side to the magazines.

Architecture, geology, surfing,

weight lifting, knitting, politics, sex. *Balling from Behind* caught his eye

(a whole magazine devoted to this?

issue after issue? year after year?) but he was too embarrassed to buy it.

He walked on. Went into a bookshop.

Browsed through the philosophy section and came to ENGLISH BOOKS ALL KINDS.

Under a tower of Agatha Christie

was one Elmore Leonard (*Killshot,* he'd read it) and *Collected Verse of Walt Whitman*

in a bilingual edition.

It is not upon you alone the dark patches fall,

The dark threw its patches down upon me also,

The best I had done seemed to me blank and suspicious,

Nor is it you alone who know what it is to be evil. . . .

. . . *tu solo quien sabe lo que es ser perverso.* Geryon put evil Walt Whitman down

and opened a self-help book

whose title (*Oblivion the Price of Sanity?*) stirred his ever hopeful heart.

"Depression is one of the unknown modes of being.

There are no words for a world without a self, seen with impersonal clarity.

All language can register is the slow return

to the oblivion we call health when imagination automatically recolors the landscape

and habit blurs perception and language

takes up its routine flourishes." He was about to turn the page for more help

when a sound caught him.

Like kissing. He looked around. A workman stood halfway up a ladder outside

the front window of the shop.

Some dark-colored bird was swooping at him and each time the bird came near

the man made a kissing noise with his mouth—

the bird somersaulted upwards then dove again with a little swagger and a cry.

Kissing makes them happy, thought Geryon

and a sense of fruitlessness pierced him. He turned to go and bumped hard

into the shoulder of a man

standing next to him—*Oh!* The stale black taste of leather filled his nose and lips.

I'm sorry—

Geryon's heart stopped. The man was Herakles. After all these years—he picks

a day when my face is puffy!

XXXIII. FAST-FORWARD

That was a shocker, they agreed over coffee at Café Mitwelt later the same day.

––––––––

Geryon couldn't decide which was more odd—

to be sitting across the table from a grown-up Herakles or to hear himself using

expressions like "a shocker."

And what about this young man with black eyebrows who sat on Herakles' left.

They do have a language, Ancash was saying.

Herakles had explained that he and Ancash were traveling around South America

together recording volcanoes.

It's for a movie, Herakles added. *A nature film? Not exactly. A documentary*

on Emily Dickinson.

Of course, said Geryon. He was trying to fit this Herakles onto the one he knew.

"On My Volcano Grows the Grass,"

Herakles went on, *is one of her poems. Yes I know,* said Geryon, *I like that poem,*

I like the way she

refuses to rhyme sod *with* God. Ancash meanwhile was taking a tape recorder

out of his pocket.

He slipped a tape into it and offered the earphones to Geryon. *Listen to this,* he said.

It's Mount Pinatubo in the Philippines.

We were there last winter. Geryon put the earphones on. Heard a hoarse animal

spraying pain from the back of its throat.

Then heavy irregular bumping sounds like tractor tires rolling downhill.

Herakles was watching.

Do you hear the rain? he said. *Rain?* Geryon adjusted the earphones. The sound

was hot as a color inside.

It was monsoon season, said Herakles, *volcanic ash and fire were mixing in midair*
with the rain. We saw villagers
racing downhill and a black wall of hot mud behind them twenty meters high,
that's what you hear on the tape.
It sort of rustles as it moves because it's full of boiling chunks of solid rock.
Geryon listened to the boiling rocks.
He also heard broken sounds like glassware snapping which he realized were
human cries and then gunshots.
Gunshots? he asked. *They had to send the army in,* said Herakles. *Even with*
lava coming down the hills at
ninety kilometers some people didn't want to leave their homes— Oh here
listen, Ancash interrupted.
He was fast-forwarding the tape then restarted it. Listen to this. Geryon listened.
Heard again the ripe animal growl.
But then came some solid thuds like melons hitting the ground. He looked at Ancash.
Up high the air gets so hot it burns
the wings off birds—they just fall. Ancash stopped. He and Geryon were looking
straight into each other's eyes.
At the word *wings* something passed between them like a vibration.
Ancash was fast-forwarding again.
About here—I think, yes—is the part from Japan. Listen it's a tsunami—
a hundred kilometers from crest to crest
when it hit the beach. We saw fishing boats carried inland as far as the next village.
Geryon listened to water destroying
a beach in Japan. Ancash was talking of continental plates. *It's worst at the edges*
of ocean trenches, where one
continental plate sinks under another. Aftershocks can go on for years.

I know, said Geryon. Herakles' gaze

on him was like a gold tongue. Magma rising. *Beg your pardon?* said Ancash.

But Geryon was taking the earphones off

and reaching for the belt of his coat. *Got to go.* The effort it took to pull himself

away from Herakles' eyes

could have been measured on the scale devised by Richter. *Call us*

we're at the City Hotel, said Herakles.

The Richter scale has neither a minimum nor a maximum threshold.

Everything depends on

the sensitivity of the seismograph. *Sure okay,* said Geryon, and threw himself

out the door.

XXXIV. HARRODS

Geryon sat in his hotel room on the end of the bed staring at the blank TV screen.

————

It was seven a.m. Total agitation possessed him. He had held off phoning Herakles

for two days. Even now he was not

looking at the telephone (which he had placed in the bottom of his sock drawer).

He was not

thinking about the two of them in their hotel room on the other side of Plaza de Mayo.

He was not

remembering how Herakles liked to make love early in the morning like a sleepy bear

taking the lid off a jar of honey– Geryon

got up suddenly and went into the bathroom. Removed his overcoat and turned on

the shower. Stood under cold water

for a minute and a half while a fragment of Emily Dickinson chased around in his head.

I never have

taken a

peach in my

Hand so late

in the Year. . . .

Why a peach? he was wondering when from deep in its cave of socks the telephone

rang. Geryon dove for it.

Geryon? That you? Hungry? said Herakles' voice. So an hour later he found himself

sitting across the table from Ancash

amid the morning carnival of Café Mitwelt. Herakles had gone for a newspaper.

Ancash sat very straight,

a man as beautiful as a live feather. *Your name—what does it mean, is it Spanish?*

No it is a Quechua word. Quechua?

Quechua is spoken in the Andes. It is one of the oldest indigenous languages of Peru.

You're from Peru?

From Huaraz. Where is that? Huaraz is in the mountains north of Lima.

You were born there?

No, Huaraz is the town of my mother. I was born in Lima. My father was a priest

who wanted to become a bishop so

my mother took me back to the mountains. Ancash smiled. *As Herakles would say,*

Such is life in the tropics.

Herakles appeared, ruffling Geryon's hair as he came past. *Who me?*

he said sitting down.

But Geryon was looking at Ancash. *Is she still there in Huaraz your mother?*

No. The terrorists were blowing up cars

and TV stations in that part of the mountains last winter. She got angry.

Death is stupid, *she said and went back to Lima.*

Does she like Lima? No one likes Lima. But how does she live? Is she alone?

Not really. She cooks for

a couple of rich people five days a week—some gringo anthropologist from the States

and his wife.

The guy is paying her to teach him Quechua. He lets her live on the roof of his house.

The roof? In Lima they use everything.

Quechua? I know some Quechua, Herakles put in brightly. Ancash gave him a raw look.

Herakles continued,

It's a song but I don't know the music just the words maybe I'll make up the music.

He started to sing. His voice rose

and fell around the strange syllables like a child's. Geryon watched him uneasily.
The voice flowed out like a fragrance
released in rain.

> *Cupi checa cupi checa*
>
> *varmi in yana yacu*
>
> *cupi checa cupi checa*
>
> *apacheta runa sapan*
>
> *cupi checa*
>
> *in ancash puru*
>
> *cupi chec*
>
> *in sillutambo*
>
> *cupi checa*
>
> *cupi checa.*

When he finished Herakles grinned at Geryon and said, *The "cupi checa" song.*
Ancash taught it to me.
Want to know what the words mean? Geryon merely nodded. *Cupi checa,*
Herakles began,
that means, right left right left– Ancash's chair which had tilted backward
on two legs came crashing forward.
Let's do Quechua lessons another time, I want to get to the post office before noon.
Soon they were out on the street
walking fast along Avenida Bolívar with a hard wind strumming their bodies,
Herakles jumping ahead like a dog
smelling everything and pointing at objects in the shops. Ancash and Geryon
came behind.

Aren't you cold? said Geryon to Ancash who had no coat on. *No,* said Ancash.
Then he looked sideways at Geryon.
Well actually yes. He smiled. Geryon would have liked to wrap his coat around
this feather man. They walked on
bent against the wind. A winter sun had thrown its bleak wares on the sky
and people going past
looked dazzled. Two women in furs came towards them swaying on their heels
like big gold foxes. No—
they are men, Geryon saw as they passed. Ancash was staring too. The foxes
disappeared into the crowd.
Ancash and Geryon walked on. Now a hunger was walking with them. *That song*
Herakles sang, Geryon said,
I heard your name in the middle of it—in ancash puru—*is that right?*
You have a good ear, said Ancash.
What does it mean? said Geryon. Ancash hesitated. *Hard to translate.* Ancash
is something like—
But Herakles whirled towards them waving his arms. *Here!* he cried pointing
at a very large department store
with deep red awnings. *Harrods of London* said the brass letters over the door.
Herakles had
vanished through the revolving door. Geryon and Ancash followed. Then stopped.
Inside Harrods life was at pause.
In a numb gray twilight salesgirls floated like survivors of a wreck. There were no
customers. The aisles smelled of tea.
Deep in the display cases a few chill objects lay stranded on dusty sateen.
Lumps of English air exhaled
from biscuit tins and moved aimlessly about the room causing sudden faded spots.

One very brightly lit case held

clocks and watches all furiously ticking, all registering quarter past six.

Geryon saw a head moving

up the escalator. *Come on,* he said to Ancash. *He always knows where to find*

the bathrooms. Ancash nodded.

At the top of the escalator they made their way around a pyramid of jellied tongue

and rubber boots and there was Herakles

on the other side of the store waving wildly. *Show you something! Over here!*

They would discuss for days after

what they had seen against the back wall of the second floor of Harrods.

Except for tongue and boots

the second floor is virtually deserted. But hovering in shadow this presence:

a circus carousel with six full-sized

wooden animals hitched to gold and silver posts on a crippled baize roulette.

The lion and the white pony are still

upright and foaming forward. The zebra, elephant, tiger, and black bear lie

toppled from harness, gazing skyward.

It's a nursery, said Herakles. *It's the etymology of Argentina,* said Ancash.

Geryon was kneeling down beside the zebra.

Want to try stealing the tiger? Looks like it's loose, said Herakles.

No one answered.

Ancash was watching Geryon. He knelt down too. Geryon was memorizing

the zebra so he could make

a photograph later. "Time Lapse." He touched his fingertips to the silk

of the eyelashes each one set

individually into its wooden sprocket in the painted eyelid above a burning eye.

Made in Germany I bet, said Ancash,

look at the workmanship.

Geryon turned to Ancash as if remembering who he was. *Can I photograph you later?*

Geryon said.

Just then a tiny refracted Herakles appeared in the staring glass of the eyeball.

Standing above them Herakles said,

Ancash I want to take the tiger to your mother. Especially if we'll be there
for her birthday—

perfect gift! What's the word for tiger *in Quechua? You told me once but I forgot.*

Tezca, said Ancash getting to his feet.

Tezca that's it Tezca the tiger god. But he has another name doesn't he?

Many names—

Herakles what are you doing? Herakles was hoisting the tiger from the floor.

With a pocketknife he began cutting

at the thick leather reins which still bound the tiger to its circus habits.

Okay Herakles suppose we do

*get it out of Harrods—*Ancash spoke reasonably—*what about the airport?*

Does it strike you

Aeroperu may object to a life-sized wooden circus animal boarding their plane?

Don't be irreverent, Herakles panted,

he's not a wooden circus animal he's Tezca the tiger god. He can go on as baggage.

Baggage?

We'll wrap him in a gun bag lots of people take guns to Peru.

Ancash sat down on the edge of the carousel

resting his arms on his knees. Ancash watched Herakles.

Geryon watched Ancash.

He was in an inward fury—So they're off to Peru leaving me here without

a backward glance—when a dull clank

came down on a shuddering sound. Harrods went dark. Geryon heard

a low voice say, *He always knows where to find the fusebox.*

Alarms went off all over the store and Herakles ran up and then the three of them

were hoisting the tiger onto his shoulders

and heading for the escalator. *Vamos hombres!* yelled Herakles. And so

they went to Peru.

XXXV. GLADYS

Not only was he very hungry but much more humiliating—

———

12,000 meters above the mountains that divide Argentina from Chile

with their long white gouges tracing

the red sandstone like a meringue pie—Geryon felt himself becoming aroused.

He was sitting in between Herakles and Ancash.

The plane was cold and they had an Aeroperu blanket thrown over

the three of them. Geryon was trying to read.

He had not realized until he found himself stranded in it high above the Andes

halfway to Lima that the novel he'd bought

in the Buenos Aires airport was pornographic. It made him furious with himself

to be stirred by dull sentences like,

Gladys slid a hand under her nightgown and began to caress her own thighs. Gladys!

He loathed the name. But his thighs

under the Aeroperu blanket were very warm. He snapped off the light

and shoved the book deep out of sight

in the seat pocket ahead of him. Sat back in the dark. On his left side Herakles

stirred in sleep. Ancash was motionless

on the right. Geryon tried to cross his knees but could not, then shifted sideways

to the left. He would pretend to be asleep

so he could lean against Herakles' shoulder. The smell of the leather jacket near

his face and the hard pressure of Herakles'

arm under the leather sent a wave of longing as strong as a color through Geryon.

It exploded at the bottom of his belly.

Then the blanket shifted. He felt Herakles' hand move on his thigh and Geryon's head went back like a poppy in a breeze

as Herakles' mouth came down on his and blackness sank through him. Herakles'

hand was on his zipper. Geryon gave himself up

to pleasure as the aeroplane moved at 978 kilometers per hour through clouds

registering −57 degrees centigrade.

Two women with toothbrushes stumbled up the aisle in the reddish dawn dark.

These are all very fine passengers,

thought Geryon dreamily as he and the plane began descent to Lima. It filled him

with tenderness to see many of the people

had little red flush marks on their cheeks where they had slept with faces

pressed to the seat cushion. Gladys!

XXXVI. ROOF

A soiled white Saturday morning in Lima.

————

The sky heavy and dark as if before rain but it hasn't rained in Lima since 1940.
On the roof of the house Geryon stood
looking out to sea. Chimneys and lines of laundry surrounded him on all sides.
Everything curiously quiet.
On the roof next door a man in black silk kimono emerged at the top of a ladder.
Clutching his kimono around him
he stepped onto the roof and stood motionless in front of a big rusted water tank.
Stared hard at the tank then lifted
the brick holding down the lid and peered inside. Replaced the brick. Went back
down the ladder. Geryon turned
to see Ancash climbing up onto the roof. *Buenos días,* said Ancash. *Hi,* said Geryon.
Their eyes failed to meet.
You slept well? asked Ancash. *Yes thank you.* They had all three slept on the roof
in sleeping bags borrowed
from the American downstairs. Ancash's mother had the roof divided into living,
sleeping and horticultural areas.
Beside the water tank was where guests slept. Next to that was "Ancash's room,"
an area bordered on one side by the clothesline,
where Ancash had neatly arranged his T-shirts on hangers, and on the other side
by a scarred highboy inlaid with mother-of-pearl.
Beside the highboy was the library. Here were two sofas and a bookcase packed
with books. On the writing desk stood
piles of paper weighted down with tins of tobacco and a gooseneck reading lamp

————————

that plugged into a cracked extension cord

running across the desk and over the roof and down the ladder to the kitchen.

Ancash had made a ceiling of palm fronds

above the library. They moved and clicked in the wind like wooden tongues.

Next to the library was a squat structure

built of clear heavy plastic and some pieces of dismantled telephone booth.

Here Ancash's mother grew a cash crop

of marijuana and herbs for cooking. She called it Festinito ("Little Feast")

and said it was her favorite place

in the world. Plaster figures of St. Francis and St. Rose of Lima were placed

encouragingly among the plants.

She herself slept next to the Little Feast on a cot piled high with bright blankets.

You were not cold? Ancash continued.

Oh no just fine, said Geryon. In fact he had never been so cold in his life as last night

under the dull red winter stars of Lima.

Ancash came over to the edge of the roof and stood beside Geryon staring down

towards the streets and the sea.

Geryon stared too. Sounds came to them across the white air. There was the slow

thock of a hammer. An uncertain music

like a water pipe starting and stopping. Many layers of traffic. A crackle of garbage

burning. Dry howls of dogs. Sounds

entered Geryon small at first but gradually filling his mind. The streets below

were after all not empty. Two men crouched

beside a half-built wall pulling bricks out of a little stone oven on a shovel.

A boy was sweeping the steps of the church

with a palm frond as big as himself. A man and woman stood eating breakfast

out of plastic containers and staring

///////

in opposite directions up and down the street. They had a thermos and two cups
perched on the hood of their car.

Five policemen strolled past with carbines. Down on the beach a soccer team was
practicing and beyond them

the filthy Pacific came crashing in. *It is different from Argentina,* said Geryon.
How do you mean?

No one here is in a hurry. Ancash smiled but said nothing. *They move so softly,*
Geryon added. He was watching the soccer team

whose movements had the rounded languor of a dream. Smells of burning blew across
the air. Dogs went nosing without urgency

through the garbage and marigolds that lined the seawall. *You're right Argentinians
are much faster. Always going somewhere.*

Geryon could see many small Peruvian people wandering along the seawall. Often they
would stop to stare at nothing in particular.

Everyone seems to be waiting, said Geryon. *Waiting for what?* said Ancash.
Yes waiting for what, said Geryon.

There was a sudden loud hiss. The electrical cord that ran across the roof
at their feet exploded in light sparks.

Damn, said Ancash. *I wish she'd rewire this. Every time someone plugs in the kettle
in the kitchen we have a meltdown.*

Herakles' head appeared on the ladder. *Hombres!* He clambered up onto the roof.
Big chunk of papaya in his hand which he waved at Geryon.

You should try this stuff Geryon! It's like eating the sun! Herakles sank his mouth
into the fruit and grinned at them.

Juice ran down his face and onto his bare chest. Geryon watched a drop of sun
slide past Herakles' nipple and over his belly

and vanish into the top of his jeans. He moved his eyes away. *Did you see the parrots?*

Herakles demanded.

Parrots? said Geryon. *Yes she has a room full of parrots at the front of the house.*
Must be fifty birds in there.
Purple green orange blue yellow it's like an explosion and there's one big
motherfucker who's totally gold. Says
she's going to have to get rid of it. Why? asked Geryon. *Kills everything smaller*
than itself. Last week it killed the cat.
That's conjecture, Ancash interrupted. *No one saw it kill the cat. Whose cat?*
asked Geryon rather lost.
Marguerite's, said Ancash. *Marguerite is the wife of the American downstairs*
you remember she lent us the sleeping bags
last night? Oh, said Geryon, *the woman with the cold hands.* He barely recalled
introductions in a foggy kitchen at four a.m.
Thing is, who else would have killed the cat? Herakles persisted. *Guerrillas maybe,*
said Ancash. *Last winter they killed*
all the cats in Huaraz one weekend. Why? said Geryon. *A gesture,* said Ancash.
Gesture of what? said Geryon.
Well it was after a TV broadcast where the president spoke from his living room.
He sat in an armchair with a cat
on his lap explaining how the police had the terrorists completely under control.
Next day no cats.
Good thing he didn't have his wife on his lap, said Herakles licking his chin.
The electrical cord was sparking again.
A little black puff rose from it. *Want me to fix that?* said Herakles as he
wiped his hands on his jeans.
Okay, said Ancash, *my mother would appreciate it. Got any duct tape?* said Herakles.
I don't know let's go look in the kitchen.

~~~~~~~~

They disappeared down the ladder. Geryon closed his eyes a moment, pulling

his overcoat tight around him.

The wind had changed, now blowing in from the sea and carrying a raw smell.

Geryon was cold. Hungry. His body

felt like a locked box. Lima is terrible, he thought, why am I here? Overhead

the sky waited too.

XXXVII. EYEWITNESSES

Saturday went whitely on.

———————

Geryon walked along the seawall. He passed groups of people waiting
and individuals waiting.
There was neither excitement nor the absence of excitement. Dogs waited.
Police waited resting their guns
against a parked car. The soccer team had withdrawn from the beach to wait
on a verandah overlooking the seawall.
While waiting most people gazed steadily out to sea or down the street. A few
kicked stones. Geryon started back
to the house. From a block away he could hear the parrots. No one was home.
He went up to the roof and sat
on his cot trying to think how to photograph Lima. But his brain was as blank
as the featureless sky.
He went out walking again. Along the seawall. Past many small shut houses.
Down alleyways where stinging sea fog
hung in clots over the cobblestones. Across a ragged park where two llamas
were tethered beside a gigantic bronze head,
its mouth open in an O as when someone dies laughing. Geryon sat in the mouth
dangling his feet and eating a banana
while the llamas pulled at the sparse grass. Mental states like anxiety or grief
have degrees, he thought, but boredom
has no degrees. *I shall never amount to much,* he remarked to the llamas.
They did not look up.
Geryon tossed his half-eaten banana onto the ground near them. They nosed it

out of the way and kept on pulling grass.

Geryon saw night was coming on. He climbed out of the mouth and went his way.

Back along the seawall towards the house

with the chicken-wired front window where fifty red parrots dove and roared

like a conscious waterfall. That would be

a good title for the photograph, Geryon thought as he strode along. Night always

perked him up.

Many hours later Geryon was sitting on his cot on the roof thinking about sleep but

too cold to move. Ancash appeared

on the ladder with his blankets in his arms. Piled them on the floor by Geryon.

I will show you how to keep warm

on a winter night in Lima, said Ancash. *It's very simple the important thing is*

do you need to take a piss?

Because once I wrap you up you'll have to stay that way till morning.

No I'm okay but—

Good then come over here and take off your overcoat.

Take off what?—said Herakles jumping

off the ladder. *You*

having a party up here without me?

Ancash was unfolding a blanket.

I'm showing Geryon a way to stay warm for the night, he said. Herakles came

towards them grinning.

I could show him some ways to stay warm for the night. Geryon paused like a hare

in headlights.

Ancash took a step. *Why don't you let things be,* he said to Herakles.

There was a moment of thick silence.

Then Herakles shrugged and turned away. *Okay,* he said. *I'll go down and smoke dope with your mother.*

My mother doesn't smoke dope she only sells it, said Ancash to Herakles' back.

And she'll make you pay.

We'll see, said Herakles and vanished down the ladder. Ancash looked at Geryon.

Difficult man, he said.

He held up the blanket. Geryon looked on numbly.

Okay now off with your coat

and then take hold of this end while I wrap the rest of it around you, said Ancash

holding out the blanket.

It's pure wool it will trap all your body heat if we wind it right come on Geryon

you'll have to lift your—

Listen Ancash, Geryon broke in, *this is great I really appreciate it but I think*

it'd be better if you just

leave the blankets here and let me do it myself—

Don't be stupid Geryon

how can you do it yourself? It has to go all the way around you two or three times

then you lie down and I pile the others on top—

No really Ancash I don't—

Geryon sometimes you try my patience just do it okay? Just give me the benefit

of the doubt here I've had a very long day.

Ancash stepped forward and pulled Geryon's overcoat down past his shoulders

and off his arms. It fell to the floor.

Then he thrust the blanket into Geryon's hands and spun him around so he could

start wrapping from the back.

All of a sudden the night was a bowl of silence. *Jesus Mary and Joseph,*

said Ancash quietly.

He gave a low whistle. Ancash had not seen Geryon's wings before.

‒ ‒ ‒ ‒ ‒ ‒ ‒

They rustled through the two slits

cut in the back of Geryon's T-shirt and sank a bit on the night wind.

Ancash ran his fingers slowly

down the red struts that articulated each wing base. Geryon shivered.

He wondered if he was going to faint.

Yazcamac, whispered Ancash. He took Geryon by the arms and rotated him

to face front. *I beg your pardon?* said Geryon

in a faraway voice. *Here sit down we have to talk.* Ancash pushed Geryon down

on the cot. He picked a blanket

off the floor and threw it around Geryon's shoulders then sat beside him.

Thanks, mumbled Geryon

pulling the blanket over his head. *Now listen to me Geryon,*

Ancash was saying,

there's a village in the mountains north of Huaraz called Jucu and in Jucu

they believe some strange things.

It's a volcanic region. Not active now. In ancient times they worshipped

the volcano as a god and even

threw people into it. For sacrifice? asked Geryon whose head had come out

of the blanket.

No not exactly. More like a testing procedure. They were looking for people

from the inside. Wise ones.

Holy men I guess you would say. The word in Quechua is Yazcol Yazcamac *it means*

the Ones Who Went and Saw and Came Back—

I think the anthropologists say eyewitnesses. *These people did exist.*

Stories are told of them still.

Eyewitnesses, said Geryon.

Yes. People who saw the inside of the volcano.

And came back.

Yes.

How do they come back?

Wings.

Wings? Yes that's what they say the Yazcamac return as red people with wings,
all their weaknesses burned away—

and their mortality. What's wrong Geryon? Geryon was scratching furiously.
Something biting me, he said.

*Oh shit I wonder where that blanket's been. Here—*Ancash pulled it off—
give it to me. *Probably*

parrot ticks those birds are—Hombres! said Herakles bounding up the ladder.
Guess what? We're going to Huaraz!

Your mother wants to show me the town! Ancash stared dumbly at Herakles
who didn't notice but

fell onto the cot beside Geryon. *We're going to see the high Andes Geryon!*
first thing tomorrow

I'll get a rental car and we'll start. Be there by dark she says. Marguerite
is giving your mom the day off

he said turning to Ancash, *so we can stay all weekend come back Sunday night—*
what do you think?

He grinned at Ancash. *Think you're quite an operator is what I think.*

Yeah! Herakles laughed

and flicked Geryon's blanket. *I'm a master of monsters aren't I?*

He grabbed Geryon

and tumbled him back onto the cot. *Fuck off Herakles,* Geryon's voice came out
muffled from under Herakles' arm.

But Herakles jumped up—*Have to call the rental place—*and rushed down the ladder.

Ancash watched Geryon in silence

as he gathered himself to the edge of the cot and sat slowly upright.

Geryon you'll have to be careful in Huaraz.

There are people around there still looking for eyewitnesses. If you see someone
checking your shadow

you come get me, okay? He smiled. *Okay.* Geryon almost smiled.

Ancash paused.

And listen if you're cold tonight you can sleep with me. With a look he added,

Just sleep. He left.

Geryon sat staring out over the roofs into the darkness. The Pacific at night is red
and gives off a soot of desire.

Every ten meters or so along the seawall Geryon could see small twined couples.
They looked like dolls.

Geryon wished he could envy them but he did not. I have to get out of this place,
he thought. Immortal or not.

He climbed into his sleeping bag and slept until dawn without moving.

XXXVIII. CAR

Geryon sat in the back seat watching the edge of Herakles' face.

He had dreamed of thorns. A forest of huge blackish-brown thorn trees
where creatures that looked
like young dinosaurs (yet they were strangely lovely) went crashing
through underbrush and tore
their hides which fell behind them in long red strips. He would call
the photograph "Human Valentines."
Herakles in the front seat rolled down his window to buy a tamale.
They were driving
through downtown Lima. At each traffic light the car was surrounded
by a swarm of children
selling food, cassettes, crucifixes, American dollar bills, and Inca Kola.
Vamos! shouted Herakles
pushing the arms of several children out of the car as Ancash's mother
shifted gears and shot the car ahead.
Bright smells of tamale filled the car. Ancash sank back to sleep
with his head against
a thick knot of greasy cloth plugging one of the holes in the side of the car.
Got an air-conditioned one!
Herakles had announced with a grin when he returned from the rental place.
Ancash's mother said nothing,
as was her custom, but motioned him out of the driver's seat. Then she
took the wheel and off they went.
They drove for hours through the filthy white sludge of Lima suburbs

where houses were bags of cement

piled up to a cardboard roof or automobile tires in a circle with one tire

burning in the middle.

Geryon watched children in spotless uniforms with pointy white collars

emerge from the cardboard houses

and make their way along the edge of the highway laughing jumping holding

their bookbags high. Then Lima ended.

The car was enclosed in a dense fist of fog. They drove on blindly. No sign

of road or sea. The sky got dark.

Just as suddenly fog ended and they came out on an empty plateau where

sheer green walls of sugarcane

rose straight up on both sides of the car. Sugarcane ended. They drove up

and up and up and up

around switchbacks carved out of bare rock higher and higher all afternoon.

Passed one or two other cars

then they were entirely alone as the sky lifted them towards itself.

Ancash was asleep.

His mother did not speak. Herakles was strangely silent. What is he thinking?

Geryon wondered.

Geryon watched prehistoric rocks move past the car and thought about thoughts.

Even when they were lovers

he had never known what Herakles was thinking. Once in a while he would say,

Penny for your thoughts!

and it always turned out to be some odd thing like a bumper sticker or a dish

he'd eaten in a Chinese restaurant years ago.

What Geryon was thinking Herakles never asked. In the space between them

developed a dangerous cloud.

Geryon knew he must not go back into the cloud. Desire is no light thing.

He could see the thorns gleam

with their black stains. Herakles had once told him he had a fantasy

of being made love to in a car

by a man who tied his hands to the door. Perhaps he is thinking of that now,

thought Geryon as he watched

the side of Herakles' face. The car all of a sudden flew up in the air and crashed

down again onto the road.

Madonna! spat out Ancash's mother. She shifted gears as they lurched forward.

The road had been getting steadily

rockier during their ascent and now was little more than a dirt path strewn

with boulders. It seemed

that darkness had descended but then the car rounded a curve and the sky

rushed open before them—

bowl of gold where the last moments of sunset were exploding—then another curve

and blackness snuffed out all.

I really could go for a hamburger right now, Herakles announced.

Ancash moaned in his sleep.

Ancash's mother said nothing. The car passed a small cement house with no roof.

Then another. Then a huddle

of women squatting on the ground smoking cigarettes in the glare of the moon.

Huaraz, said Geryon.

XXXIX. HUARAZ

Water boils in Huaraz at seventy degrees centigrade.

———

It is very high. The altitude will set your heart jumping. The town is held in a ring
of bare sandrock mountains
but to the north rises one sudden angular fist of total snow. *Andes!* cried Herakles
as he entered the dining room.
They had stayed overnight in Huaraz' Hotel Turístico. The dining room faced north
and was so dark against
the morning light outside they were all momentarily blinded. They sat.
I think we are the only guests
in this hotel, said Geryon looking around the empty tables. Ancash nodded.
No tourism in Peru anymore.
No foreigners? No foreigners, no Peruvians either. Nobody goes north of Lima
these days. Why? said Geryon.
Fear, said Ancash. *This coffee tastes weird,* said Herakles. Ancash poured coffee
and tasted it then spoke to his mother in Quechua.
She says it's got blood in it. What do you mean blood? Cow blood, it's a local recipe. Supposed to
strengthen your heart.
Ancash leaned toward his mother and said something that made her laugh.
But Herakles was gazing out the window.
This light is amazing! he said *Looks like TV!* Now he was putting on his jacket.
Who wants to go exploring?
Soon they were proceeding up the main street of Huaraz. It rises in sharp relations
of light towards the fist of snow.
Lining both sides of the street are small wooden tables where you can buy Chiclets,

/ / / / / / / /

pocket calculators, socks,

round loaves of hot bread, televisions, lengths of leather, Inca Kola, tombstones,

bananas, avocados, aspirin,

soap, AAA batteries, scrub brushes, car headlights, coconuts, American novels,

American dollars. The tables

are manned by women as small and tough as cowboys who wear layers of skirts

and a black fedora. Men wearing

dusty black suits and the fedora stand about in knots for discussion. Children

dressed in blue school uniforms

or track suits and the fedora chase around the tables. There are a few smiles,

many broken teeth, no anger.

Ancash and his mother were speaking Quechua all the time now or else Spanish

with Herakles. Geryon kept

the camera in his hand and spoke little. I am disappearing, he thought

but the photographs were worth it.

A volcano is not a mountain like others. Raising a camera to one's face has effects

no one can calculate in advance.

XL. PHOTOGRAPHS: ORIGIN OF TIME

It is a photograph of four people sitting around a table with hands in front of them.

———

The pipe glows on a small clay bowl

in the middle. Beside it a kerosene lamp. Monstrous rectangles flare up the walls.

I will call it "Origin of Time,"

thought Geryon as a terrible coldness came through the room from somewhere.

It was taking him a very long while

to set up the camera. Enormous pools of a moment kept opening around his hands

each time he tried to move them.

Coldness was planing the sides off his vision leaving a narrow canal down which

the shock— Geryon sat

on the floor suddenly. He had never been so stoned in his life. I am too naked,

he thought. This thought seemed profound.

And I want to be in love with someone. This too fell on him deeply. It is all wrong.

Wrongness came like a lone finger

chopping through the room and he ducked. *What was that?* said one of the others

turning towards him centuries later.

XLI. PHOTOGRAPHS: JEATS

It is a close-up photograph of Geryon's left pant leg just below the knee.

———

Resting the camera on the rear window of the car Geryon is watching the road

fall away behind them

into a light so brilliant it feels cold and hot at once. The car hurtles over gravel

and rock traveling

almost vertically on the steep mountain track that leads up to Icchantikas.

Car travel gives some people hemorrhoids.

Each time the car bounces him up and down Geryon utters a little red cry.

No one hears him.

Herakles and Ancash in the front seat are (in English) discussing Yeats which

Ancash pronounces Jeats.

Not Jeats. Yeats, says Herakles. *What? Yeats not Jeats. Sounds the same to me.*

It's like the difference between Jell-O and yellow.

Jellow?

Herakles sighs.

English is a bitch, Ancash's mother announces unexpectedly from the back seat

and that closes it—

Ancash hits the brakes and the car jumps to a halt. Geryon's hot apple icepicks

all the way up his anus to his spine

as four soldiers appear from nowhere to surround the car. Geryon is focusing

the camera on their guns

when Ancash's mother slides her left hand over the shutter and gently forces it

out of sight between Geryon's knees.

XLII. PHOTOGRAPHS: THE MEEK

It is a photograph of two burros grazing on spiky grass in a stubble field.

———

What is it about burros?
Geryon is thinking. Except burros there is not much to see out the car window
as he and the mother sit
waiting in the back seat. The police have taken Ancash and Herakles down the road
and vanished into a little adobe house.
The burros seek and munch with their long silk ears angled towards the hot sky.
Their necks and knobby knees
make Geryon sad. No not sad, he decides, but what? Ancash's mother says a few
fast harsh Spanish words
out her side of the car. She seems to be stating her mind boldly today, perhaps
he will do the same.
What is it about burros? he says aloud. *Guess they're waiting to inherit the earth,*
she answers him in English
with a little rough laugh that he thinks about all the rest of the day.

XLIII. PHOTOGRAPHS: I AM A BEAST

It is a photograph of a guinea pig lying on her right side on a plate.

———

She is surrounded by cabbage salad and large round slices of yam.

Two perfect tiny white teeth

project over her blackened lower lip. Her flesh still sizzling from the oven

gives off a hot glow and her left eye

is looking straight up at Geryon. He taps the flank twice shyly with his fork

then sets the utensil down

and waits for the meal to be over. Meanwhile Herakles and Ancash and the mother

and the four soldiers

(who invited them all for lunch) are chopping and chewing with gusto. Geryon

studies the room. Noon shadows

shift down from a light hole cut in the roof. A big black iron stove still crackles.

The floor is covered with mats

of woven palm and a few survivor guinea pigs are gamboling about near the stove.

Propped on three Inca Kola crates

facing the table is the TV. *Jeopardy!* is on, volume low. Four guns rest by the door.

Icchantikas is active yes

(one of the soldiers is telling Herakles) *you'll see when you get to Jucu.*

The town is built into the slope

of the volcano—there are holes in the wall you can look through and see the fire.

They use them to bake bread.

I don't believe you, says Herakles. The soldier shrugs. Ancash's mother looks up.

No it's true, she says. *Lava bread.*

Makes you passionate. A greasy grin passes around the soldiers.

———————

What does it mean, Icchantikas? asks Geryon.

Ancash looks at his mother. She says something in Quechua. Ancash turns to Geryon

but one of the soldiers interrupts

speaking in fast Spanish to Ancash's mother. She watches the soldier a moment

then shoves back her chair.

Muchas gracias hombres, she says. *We go.* In the cooling left eye of the guinea pig

they all stand reflected

pulling out their chairs and shaking hands. The eye empties.

XLIV. PHOTOGRAPHS: THE OLD DAYS

It is a photograph of a man's naked back, long and bluish.

―――――

Herakles standing at the window staring out on the dark before dawn.

When they made love

Geryon liked to touch in slow succession each of the bones of Herakles' back

as it arched away from him into

who knows what dark dream of its own, running both hands all the way down

from the base of the neck

to the end of the spine which he can cause to shiver like a root in the rain.

Herakles makes

a low sound and moves his head on the pillow, slowly opens his eyes.

He starts.

Geryon what's wrong? Jesus I hate it when you cry. What is it?

Geryon thinks hard.

I once loved you, now I don't know you at all. He does not say this.

I was thinking about time—he gropes—

you know how apart people are in time together and apart at the same time—stops.

Herakles wipes tears from Geryon's face

with one hand. *Can't you ever just fuck and not think?* Herakles gets out of bed

and goes into the bathroom.

Then he comes back and stands at the window a long while. By the time he returns

to the bed it is getting light.

Well Geryon just another Saturday morning me laughing and you crying,

he says as he climbs in.

Geryon watches him pull the blanket up to his chin. *Just like the old days.*

Just like the old days, Geryon says too.

///////

XLV. PHOTOGRAPHS:
LIKE AND NOT LIKE

It was a photograph just like the old days. Or was it?

———

He slid off the bed quickly. Thorns all around him black and glistening

but he passed through unhurt

and out the door pulling his overcoat around him as he went. Corridor deserted

except for a red EXIT sign at the end.

Pressing hard on the spring bar of the door he stepped out into a blood-colored dawn.

Not the parking lot. He was in the debris

of the hotel garden. Ruined roses of every variety paused stiffly on their stalks.

Dry blades of winter fennel clicked

in the cold air and swung low over the ground shedding feathery gold stuff.

What is that smell?

Geryon was thinking and then he saw Ancash. At the bottom of the garden on a bench

built into a big pine tree. Sitting

motionless with knees under his chin and arms folded on his knees. Eyes stayed

on Geryon as he crossed the garden,

hesitated then sat down on the ground in front of the bench. *'Día,* said Geryon.

Ancash regarded him silently.

Look as if you didn't sleep much, said Geryon.

. . . .

Kind of cold out here aren't you cold just sitting still?

. . . .

Maybe we could go get some breakfast.

. . . .

Or just walk downtown sure would like some coffee.

. . . .

Geryon studied the ground in front of him for a while. Drew a small diagram

in the dirt with his finger.

Looked up. His eyes met Ancash's eyes and they both rose at once and Ancash hit

Geryon as hard as he could

across the face with the flat of his hand. Geryon stumbled backwards and Ancash hit

him again with the other hand

knocking Geryon to his knees. He's ambidextrous! thought Geryon with admiration

as he scrambled to his feet swinging

wildly. He would have landed a punch on the pine tree and broken his hand

had Ancash not caught him.

They swayed together and balanced. Then Ancash unlaced his arms and stood back.

With the front of his shirt

he wiped snot and blood from Geryon's face. *Sit,* he said pushing Geryon to the bench.

Put your head back.

Geryon sat and leaned his head against the trunk of the tree.

Don't swallow, said Ancash.

Geryon stared up through pine branches at Venus. All the same, he thought, I'd like

to punch someone.

So, said Ancash daubing at the bright purple mark on Geryon's right cheekbone.

Geryon waited.

You love him? Geryon thought about that. *In my dreams I do. Your dreams?*

Dreams of the old days.

When you first knew him? Yes, when I—knew him.

What about now?

Yes—no—I don't know. Geryon pressed his hands over his face then let them fall.

No it's not there now.

They were quiet awhile then Ancash said, *So.*

Geryon waited.

So what's it like–Ancash stopped. He began again. *So what's it like fucking him now?*

Degrading, said Geryon

without a pause and saw Ancash recoil from the word.

I'm sorry I shouldn't have said that,

said Geryon but Ancash was gone across the garden. At the door he turned.

Geryon?

Yes.

There is one thing I want from you.

Tell me.

Want to see you use those wings.

A silence tossed itself across the tall gold heads of the fennel stalks between them.

Into this silence burst Herakles.

Conchitas! he cried stepping out the exit door. *Buen' día!* Then he saw Ancash's face

and looked toward Geryon and paused.

Ah, he said. Geryon was groping in the bottom of his huge coat pocket. Ancash pushed

past Herakles. Vanished into the hotel.

Herakles looked at Geryon. *Volcano time?* he said. In the photograph the face of

Herakles is white. It is the face

of an old man. It is a photograph of the future, thought Geryon months later when he

was standing in his darkroom

looking down at the acid bath and watching likeness come groping out of the bones.

XLVI. PHOTOGRAPHS: # 1748

It is a photograph he never took, no one here took it.

———

Geryon is standing beside the bed in his overcoat watching Ancash struggle awake.

He has the tape recorder in hand.

When he sees Ancash's eyes open he says, *How long are the batteries good for?*

About three hours, Ancash answers

sleepily from the pillow. *Why? What are you up to? What time is it anyway?*

About four-thirty, says Geryon, *go back to sleep.*

Ancash mumbles a word and slides back under his dream. *Want to give you*

something to remember me by,

whispers Geryon closing the door. He has not flown for years but why not

be a

black speck raking its way toward the crater of Icchantikas on icy possibles,

why not rotate

the inhuman Andes at a personal angle and retreat when it spins—if it does

and if not, win

bolts of wind like slaps of wood and the bitter red drumming of wing muscle on air—

he flicks Record.

This is for Ancash, he calls to the earth diminishing below. This is a memory of our

beauty. He peers down

at the earth heart of Icchantikas dumping all its photons out her ancient eye and he

smiles for

the camera: "The Only Secret People Keep."

XLVII. THE FLASHES IN WHICH A MAN POSSESSES HIMSELF

Flour powders the air around them and settles on their arms and eyes and hair.

———

One man shapes the dough,

the other two shovel it on long handles into a square hole filled with flames

cut into the back wall.

Herakles and Ancash and Geryon have stopped outside the bakery to stare

at the hole of fire.

After quarreling all day they went out to walk the dark streets of Jucu.

It is a starless windless midnight.

Cold drills up from the ancient rocks below. Geryon walks behind the others.

Little spurts of acid

keep filling his mouth from two red pepper tamales eaten fast a few hours ago.

They are following the palisade.

Pass down an alley then turn a corner and there it is. Volcano in a wall.

Do you see that, says Ancash.

Beautiful, Herakles breathes out. He is looking at the men.

I mean the fire, says Ancash.

Herakles grins in the dark. Ancash watches the flames.

We are amazing beings,

Geryon is thinking. We are neighbors of fire.

And now time is rushing towards them

where they stand side by side with arms touching, immortality on their faces,

night at their back.

INTERVIEW

==========

(STESICHOROS)

I: One critic speaks of a sort of concealment drama going on in your work some special interest in finding out what or how people act when they know that important information is being withheld this might have to do with an aesthetic of blindness or even a will to blindness if that is not a tautology

s: I will tell about blindness

I: Yes do

s: First I must tell about seeing

I: Fine

s: Up to 1907 I was seriously interested in seeing I studied and practiced it I enjoyed it

I: 1907

s: I will tell about 1907

I: Please

s: First I must tell about what I saw

I: Okay

s: Paintings completely covered the walls right up to the ceiling at the time the atelier was lit by gas fixtures and it glowed like a dogma but this is not what I saw i: No

s: Naturally I saw what I saw

i: Naturally

s: I saw everything everyone saw

i: Well yes

s: No I mean everything everyone saw everyone saw because I saw it

i: Did they

s: I was (very simply) in charge of seeing for the world after all seeing is just a substance

i: How do you know that

s: I saw it

i: Where

s: Wherever I looked it poured out my eyes I was responsible for everyone's visibility it was a great pleasure it increased daily

i: A pleasure you say

s: Of course it had its disagreeable side I could not blink or the world went blind

i: So no blinking

s: No blinking from 1907 on

i: Until

s: Until the start of the war then I forgot

i: And the world

s: The world went ahead much as before let's talk about something else now

i: Description can we talk about description

s: What is the difference between a volcano and a guinea pig is not a description why is it like it is is a description ɪ: I take it you are speaking formally what about content

s: No difference

ɪ: How about your little hero Geryon

s: Exactly it is red that I like and there is a link between geology and character

ɪ: What is this link

s: I have often wondered

ɪ: Identity memory eternity your constant themes

s: And how can regret be red and might it be

ɪ: Which brings us to Helen

s: There is no Helen

ɪ: I believe our time is up

s: Thank you for this and for everything

ɪ: It is I who thank you

s: So glad you didn't ask about the little red dog

ɪ: Next time

s: That's three

A NOTE ABOUT THE AUTHOR

———

Anne Carson is an award-winning poet and essayist. She teaches Classics at McGill University in Montreal, Canada, and at the University of California, Berkeley.

A NOTE ON THE TYPE

———

The text of this book was set in Berthold Bodoni Old Face, a typeface named for Giambattista Bodoni, who was born at Saluzzo, Piedmont, in 1740. The son of a printer, Bodoni went to Rome as a young man to serve as an apprentice at the press of the Propaganda. In 1768 he was put in charge of the Stamperia reale in Parma by Duke Ferdinand, a position he held until his death in 1813. Bodoni's innovations in type style included a greater degree of contrast in the thick and thin elements of the letters and a sharper and more angular finish of details.

Composed by Dix, Syracuse, New York

Printed and bound by Quebecor Printing, Martinsburg, West Virginia

Designed by Misha Beletsky